Vitalize Your English Studies with Authentic Videos

INTEGRITY
Advanced

Osamu Takeuchi   Koichi Yamaoka
Mizuki Moriyasu   Brent Cotsworth

KINSEIDO

Kinseido Publishing Co., Ltd.

3-21 Kanda Jimbo-cho, Chiyoda-ku,
Tokyo 101-0051, Japan

First published 2023 by Kinseido Publishing Co., Ltd.

Design　　　DAITECH co., ltd.

 音声ファイル無料ダウンロード

https://www.kinsei-do.co.jp/download/4176

この教科書で 🎧 **DL 00 の表示がある箇所の音声は、上記 URL または QR コードにて**
無料でダウンロードできます。自習用音声としてご活用ください。

▶ PC からのダウンロードをお勧めします。スマートフォンなどでダウンロードされる場合は、
　　ダウンロード前に「解凍アプリ」をインストールしてください。

▶ URL は、**検索ボックスではなくアドレスバー (URL 表示欄)** に入力してください。

▶ お使いのネットワーク環境によっては、ダウンロードできない場合があります。

◎ CD 00　　左記の表示がある箇所の音声は、教室用 CD（Class Audio CD）に収録されています。

Preface

In recent years, online videos have become an integral part of daily life for many university students. Within this context, it is becoming increasingly vital that such media be used in education to excite student interest in various global topics and events, as well as to further facilitate the development of comprehension and communication skills. The three books in this series aim to provide students with next-generation texts that utilize authentic videos to integrate and enhance the four skills of English, thereby honing students' skills in both organizing and transmitting information in English.

The *INTEGRITY* series consists of three books, organized according to proficiency level as measured by TOEIC® Test: the Beginner Level is designed for the TOEIC 300–400 range, the Intermediate Level for TOEIC 400–500, and the Advanced Level for TOEIC 500–600.

As this series utilizes videos to promote deeper learning, special emphasis was placed on the selection of the videos. Across the series, several common topics were covered, including social media, AI and modern life, environmental issues, human rights issues, urban issues, gender, and life and mental health, all of which are sure to stimulate the intellectual curiosity of university students.

In addition, the series adopts a "deep-dive" approach in which each topic is carefully examined in increasing depth and from multiple perspectives. This is achieved through four phases: "Motivating Students to Learn," "Comprehension & Deeper Understanding," "Internalization & Integration," and "Output." The series is designed to first spark interest in each topic and facilitate relatively effortless content comprehension. By having students experience various topics through English, the texts provide knowledge and simultaneously facilitate critical thinking, thus vitalizing students' learning and thinking processes through both tasks and the materials themselves. At the end of each unit, students are given an opportunity to express their thoughts and opinions on the topic in English.

The writing and editing team hopes that this series will equip students with the well-balanced command of English necessary to thrive in future society.

Finally, we would like to express our sincere appreciation to the editorial team at Kinseido for their efforts in making this series possible.

Early Winter 2022

Osamu Takeuchi (Series Supervisor)
Koichi Yamaoka
Mizuki Moriyasu
Brent Cotsworth

• Unit Structure

Through the following four phases, students will be able to study a single topic from multiple perspectives and deepen their knowledge and understanding of that topic.

PHASE 1	Motivating Students to Learn

1. Getting into the Topic

This section is designed to activate background knowledge surrounding the topic covered in the unit. Students respond to questions such as fill-in-the-blank, multiple-choice, and scrambled-sentence while referring to visual information, such as graphs and photographs. The information in this section is used to assist the video viewing in the subsequent section.

2. 1st Viewing

In this section, students view a video produced by *the Guardian*—one of the world's leading media outlets—and answer short answer questions. The videos are edited to be approximately 3 to 4 minutes in length.

Note: the aim is to use both visual and auditory input to understand the main ideas and key information of the video, not to pick up every detail.

PHASE 2	Comprehension & Deeper Understanding

1. Vocabulary

Students learn key vocabulary that appears in the subsequent Reading section in a matching task. Definitions are written in simple English.

The following dictionaries were referenced for the English definitions:

Oxford Learner's Dictionary / Cambridge Dictionary / Longman Dictionary of Contemporary English / Merriam-Webster Learner's Dictionary / Collins COBUILD Advanced Dictionary of American English / Collins Online Dictionary / Oxford Dictionary of English

2. Reading

Students read a passage of approximately 450 words written in English, which provides a wealth of social and cultural background information as well as other information related to the topic presented in Phase 1. The text is also relevant to various issues facing contemporary society. Students should read between the lines and strive to grasp the essence of the issues.

3. Organizer

A partially filled table, graphically representing the contents of the reading, is presented. By filling in these blanks, students review the main points of the reading while considering the structure of the English text as a whole.

PHASE 3   Internalization & Integration

2nd Viewing

The video from Phase 1 is shown again and students answer short answer questions that require more detailed information. Students should try to make connections with what has been learned so far. Students are sure to notice that their understanding of the video is much deeper than in the 1st Viewing.

PHASE 4   Output

Output Task

Once students are able to "own" their new knowledge, they can move on to output. Students conduct a mini-research or brainstorming session on the main theme of the unit. Then, they explain what they have researched or express their own ideas in pairs. Finally, they engage in paragraph writing or presentations. Students are expected to articulate their position on a particular issue and express their opinions. Some units include interaction-based "fun activities," such as a "Become a Something Sommelier" pair-work activity (Unit 7) or a "Dear Abby" letter-writing activity (Unit 8).

All videos have been produced by *the Guardian.*

The Guardian, which began as a weekly paper called *the Manchester Guardian* in 1821, is now one of the UK's most popular daily newspapers. It is most recognized for its investigative journalism and coverage of various social issues. In addition, its vast foreign correspondence allows it to provide stories not only domestically from the UK, but also from locations across the globe. The Guardian Media Group is like the Robin Hood of journalism, devoted to integrity and "giving a voice to the powerless and holding power to account."

Advanced
Contents

UNIT 1   *Campus Life / Australia*   TIME 3:08

9   **Nicknames: Is It Hazing?**

UNIT 2   *Renewable Energy*   TIME 3:59

15   **The Global Shift to Renewable Energy**

UNIT 3   *Race / British Society*   TIME 2:35

21   **It's (Not) an Equal World After All**

UNIT 4   *Life Counseling / Relationships*   TIME 3:22

27   **The Search for a Perfect Partner**

UNIT 5   *Active Living / Traffic Safety*   TIME 4:45

33   **Bike Helmets: Are They Safe?**

UNIT 6   *Fashion / Sustainability*   TIME 3:21

39   **Green Fabrics: Toward a Sustainable Fashion Industry**

UNIT 7   *Unique Jobs / Environment*   TIME 4:43

45   **How Does Water Taste? Ask a Water Sommelier**

UNIT 8 *Modern Families* 🎬 TIME 2:45

51 Emerging Forms of Family

UNIT 9 *AI / Robot Ethics* 🎬 TIME 4:30

57 The Dark Side of Robots with Common Sense

UNIT 10 *Space Junk / Sustainability* 🎬 TIME 5:06

63 Mission to Make Space Exploration Sustainable

UNIT 11 *Art / Advertising* 🎬 TIME 3:33

69 I ♥ NY: An Enduring Legacy of Design

UNIT 12 *Modern Women* 🎬 TIME 3:47

75 Choosing to Be Childfree

UNIT 13 *Race / Culture* 🎬 TIME 5:14

81 Shedding Light on Black Cowboy History

UNIT 14 *Gender Stereotypes* 🎬 TIME 4:57

87 Women Finding Their Strength

Nicknames: Is It Hazing?

Lots of people get a nickname at some point in their life. Some people even introduce themselves using their nicknames. The names can be cute and playful, or embarassing and upsetting. But is the risk of bullying through nicknames enough to justify a university ban on them?

PHASE 1

1 | Getting into the Topic

The following are three famous people in history and their nicknames. Fill in the blanks with the appropriate words from below.

Nickname	Profession	Origin of Nickname
Richard the "1 _____"	King of England	He spent most of his life at war and was very brave. People thought his heart was like a lion's.
"2 _____" Ruth	Baseball player	He had a cute baby face. He was also called "The Bambino" for the same reason.
"3 _____" (Louis Armstrong)	Jazz musician	[One story] His mouth was big like a satchel (a school bag).

| Bambi | Lionheart | Babe | Big-ear | Lionking | Satchmo |

2 | ◼️◀ 1st Viewing

online video

Watch the video and write down the answers to the following questions.

1. What is this student's nickname?

_____

2. What does the university believe about nicknames?

_____

PHASE 2

1 | 📋 Vocabulary

Match the words with their definitions.

1. **humiliating**   [   ]   **a.** making someone look foolish in front of others

2. **prank**   [   ]   **b.** the act of physically or mentally harming a person weaker than yourself

3. **over-consumption**   [   ]

4. **tolerance**   [   ]   **c.** symbolic actions that are performed as part of a ceremony or tradition

5. **ritual**   [   ]   **d.** a place to live or stay; housing

6. **accommodation**   [   ]   **e.** a small playful trick or joke

7. **bullying**   [   ]   **f.** accepting differences even if you do not like them

                       g. taking in too much of something; for example, drinking too much alcohol

2 | 📖 Reading

🎧 DL 02   💿 CD1-02

Read the following passage.

What's in a Nickname?

"Hazing" can be described as potentially dangerous or humiliating initiation rites that new members of a social group are expected to endure. It happens in many different types of social groups all over the world, but it is particularly common in the military, criminal gangs, sports teams, and university societies and groups. It is also called "initiation" in the UK and

5 "bastardisation" in Australia, and comes in many different forms, ranging from harmless to dangerous or violent. It may be a simple prank played on the victim by senior members of a group or an impossible or humiliating task victims must complete to be allowed into the group.

There have been a number of incidents at American universities involving serious
10 injury to the victim of hazing and, in some cases, even death. Many of these deaths are related to forced over-consumption of alcohol. In 2017, for example, a 19-year-old student at Penn State University died after he was forced to drink over 18 alcoholic drinks in less than 90 minutes.

Western Sydney University (WSU) in Australia is one university that has a zero-
15 tolerance policy toward hazing. WSU administrators claimed that the nicknames given to new freshman students by their seniors are part of rituals that violate the university's anti-hazing policy. They even banned students from wearing university jumpers bearing the students' nicknames. In an email sent to all students, the university banned hazing on campus and warned that students who were caught hazing would be kicked out of their
20 accommodations.

However, many students deny that giving nicknames to new students is connected to hazing. Students on campus interviewed by the Guardian Australia say that nicknames are randomly assigned from a list at the start of the year. By calling each other by their nicknames, the students believe they can break down barriers relating to social class and
25 background, building strong bonds for life. In Australia, the concept of "mateship" is culturally important and deeply relates to friendship, equality, and loyalty. The students argue that mateship is strengthened through nicknames. The fact is, many students were surprised at the reports of hazing on WSU campuses.

Many students believe that most of the initiation rites are harmless and help build a sense
30 of community. These rituals can also encourage discipline, a characteristic that can be very important, especially in groups such as the military or sports teams. Although some say that initiations are no different to bullying, many students disagree. It is important to take the issue of hazing seriously, but universities should make sure
35 that they do not control the students' freedom and traditions too much.   436 words

Notes

ℓ 17 **jumper:** a hooded sweatshirt, jacket, or other top; [AmE] hoodie, sweater, etc.

3 |  Organizer

Complete the organizer based on the information from the reading.

Hazing	
Definition	1 _____ _____ that new members of a social group are expected to endure
Where it happens	It happens in many different types of social groups. ➡ It is particularly common in the military, 2 _____ _____ .
Other names	UK 🇬🇧 initiation Australia 🇦🇺 3 _____
Example	In 2017, a 19-year-old student at Penn State University 4 _____ after he was forced to drink over 5 _____ in less than 6 _____ .

WSU's comments AGAINST nicknames	**Students' arguments FOR nicknames**
• They claimed that the nicknames given to new freshman students by their seniors are part of 7 _____ _____ _____ . • They banned students from 8 _____ _____ bearing the students' nicknames. • They warned that students who were caught hazing would be 9 _____ _____ .	• They say that nicknames are 10 _____ _____ at the start of the year. • They believe that nicknames can 11 _____ _____ relating to 12 _____ _____ , building 13 _____ _____ . • They argue that 14 _____ is strengthened through 15 _____ .

PHASE 3

◼◀ 2nd Viewing

Watch the video again and write down the answers to the following questions.

1. What can happen to students wearing a jumper with their nickname on the back?

_____

2. How are most students' nicknames assigned?

_____

3. According to Mykonos (or Andrew), what do the nicknames do for students?

_____

PHASE 4

💬✍ Output Task (Writing / Speaking)

You have learned that the use of nicknames often divides opinion. Discuss the benefits and drawbacks of nicknames.

Step I ▶ Think of a nickname you or someone you knew had in school. Answer the following questions.

• What was the nickname and who was it given to?	
• What was the reason/story behind the nickname?	
• How did you/the person you knew feel about the nickname?	
• Thinking back on it now, was it a good experience to have had?	

Step 2 Find a partner and share your story about the nickname from school. Together, fill in the table below with reasons you think nicknames are good and bad.

✔ **Good**	
❌ **Bad**	

Step 3 Imagine you are a high school teacher. Based on your discussions and what you have learned about nicknames, write a short letter to your students on whether you would ban nicknames from your class.

Dear Students,

I recently read about a high school that totally bans the use of nicknames. I know some of you call each other by nicknames, so I have thought about what to do in our class. I have

decided _____

_____

_____

_____

_____

_____

_____

Writing Checklist

☐ Clarified his/her stance on the given theme.

☐ Gave clear reasons for this decision.

☐ Gave a concluding remark to end the letter.

Useful Expressions
- As you may already know, ...
- Please understand that ...
- Considering X, Y, and Z, I have come to the decision to *do what*
- Although some of you may ..., ...

UNIT 2

The Global Shift to Renewable Energy

Some countries have already switched a fairly large proportion of their energy sources to renewable ones, but others are lagging behind. Does shifting toward renewable energy sources mean mass unemployment? Are solar plants the silver bullet to solve the energy problem? Things seem a bit more complicated, probably requiring a more global perspective.

PHASE 1

1 Getting into the Topic

The following table shows Australia's 2019–2020 electricity generation by fuel type. Based on the information in the table, complete the sentences.

Electricity Generation in Australia

← Fossil Fuels →			← Renewables →		
		Oil 1.7% ┐	Biomass 1.3% ┐		
Coal 54.9%	Gas 20.8%		Solar 7.9%	Wind 7.7%	Hydro 5.7%

Source: energy.gov.au

1. ¹ _____ account for nearly 80% of the country's electricity generation, while ² _____ make up just a little over 20%.

2. ³ _____ accounts for the most significant share with about 55%.
    ⁴ _____ and ⁵ _____ are the two most common renewable sources, with 7.9% and 7.7% respectively.

Advanced

2 |  1st Viewing

Watch the video and write down the answers to the following questions.

1. What renewable energy sources are mentioned?

_____

2. Which countries have asked Australia to export hydrogen to them?

_____

PHASE 2

1 | Vocabulary

Match the words with their definitions.

1. lag behind   [   ]   **a.** a part of something compared to the whole

2. opposition   [   ]   **b.** disagreement with something

3. proportion   [   ]   **c.** a large area of something, such as land

4. carbon neutrality [   ]   **d.** to be behind others in progress

5. expanse   [   ]   **e.** to support something enthusiastically

6. devastating   [   ]   **f.** the state of balancing emissions and absorption of CO_2

7. embrace   [   ]   **g.** causing fatal damages to something

2 | Reading

 DL 03   CD1-03

Read the following passage.

Renewable Energy: A Team Game?

Starting in the mid-2000s, sustainability has become a huge issue on almost every major country's agenda. Most developed countries have taken action by setting goals for implementing more sustainable energy solutions, but some are having difficulties. So far, Western countries have taken the spotlight with their quick shifts to renewable energy.

5 Iceland, for example, is in the lead with nearly 100% of its electric power coming from

hydroelectric and geothermal sources. Norway, too, has been quick to adopt hydroelectricity, with over 90% of its total electric power being produced by water. But what about the Pacific? Although New Zealand sources about 80% of all its electric power from renewables such as hydro, geothermal, and wind energy, two of its close neighbors—Australia and Japan—
10 have been lagging behind in the sustainability race. The question now is: can these two nations find a new way forward?

In 2009, the Australian government expanded its sustainable energy scheme, known as the Renewable Energy Target (RET), to make about 20% of Australia's electricity supply come from renewable sources by the year 2020. This target was easily met, with new
15 solar and wind power stations being built across the country. However, as Australia was traditionally a mining country, people have expressed concerns that closing coal-fired power stations would result in mass unemployment and damage to the economy. Worried about the opposition, the government decided not to renew the RET scheme.

Meanwhile, although Japan is one of the leading energy-efficient economies, it is still a
20 big producer of CO_2 and relies heavily on fossil fuels. As of 2019, Japan was one of the top five countries to import and consume oil for energy, with fossil fuels making up 75% of its energy supply. The Japanese government has identified the need to increase the proportion of renewable energy: it has set a target to have between 36 and 38% of its electricity supply sourced from renewables by the end of 2030 and to achieve carbon neutrality by 2050. As
25 part of this project, solar plants have been appearing in the Japanese countryside. However, some environmental campaigners argue that solar plants take up a lot of space, which requires expanses of forest to be destroyed and, ironically, has a devastating effect on local wildlife.

In spite of, or possibly because of, these challenges, Japan and Australia have decided to collaborate. While Japan possesses advanced technology in hydrogen-based energy
30 production, Australia has enough hydrogen to export to other countries. If Australia could end its love affair with coal and embrace renewable energy, it could not only decrease its own carbon emissions, but also help other countries reduce theirs. Japan can also contribute to the world's sustainable energy efforts through further development
35 of its technologies. However, most of all, working together may be the key to solving each individual country's challenges.   471 words

Note

ℓ 13 **Renewable Energy Target (RET):** a scheme started in 2001, setting Australia's renewable energy target for electric power generation

Unit 2 | The Global Shift to Renewable Energy   **17**

3  Organizer

Complete the organizer based on the information from the reading.

Renewable Energy Leaders

Country	Type(s) of renewable power sources	Proportion (%)
Iceland	[1] _____ and [2] _____ energy	Nearly 100%
Norway	[3] _____ energy	[7] _____
New Zealand	[4] _____ , [5] _____ and [6] _____ energy	[8] _____

Australia and Japan

Australia	Japan

Renewable Energy Target (RET):
• expanded in 2009
• Target
  = [9] _____ % renewable energy by
  [10] _____
Examples of renewable power sources:
• solar and wind
Concerns/Opposition:
• Closing coal-fired power stations would
  result in [11] _____
  and [12] _____ .
• The government decided [13] _____
  _____ .
	Targets:
	• proportion of renewable energy
	  = [14] _____ % by 2030
	• achieve carbon neutrality by 2050
	Example of renewable power sources:
	• [15] _____
	Concerns/Opposition:
	• Solar plants take up a lot of space, which
	  requires [16] _____
	
	  and, ironically, has a devastating effect on
	  local wildlife.

Solution = [17] _____

• Japan possesses advanced technology in [18] _____ .

• Australia has [19] _____ .

PHASE 3

🔊◀ 2nd Viewing

Watch the video again and write down the answers to the following questions.

1. How many people in Australia are employed in mining thermal coal and in the renewable energy industry, respectively?

_____

2. What is expected if renewable energy is exported from Australia to such countries as Japan, South Korea, and Germany?

_____

3. According to Professor Ken Baldwin, what is preventing the energy transition to renewables in Australia?

_____

PHASE 4

💬✎ Output Task (Writing / Speaking)

Renewable energy sources have been drawing more attention around the world in recent years. What is the right course for Japan to take in this trend?

Step I ▶ Which renewable energy sources seem suitable for Japan? Write down advantages and disadvantages of two promising sources. You may use your own knowledge or do some research.

Some examples of renewable energy sources: biofuel, geothermal heat, fuel-cell, solar, wind, hydro

Energy Source	Advantages	Disadvantages
e.g., geothermal energy	e.g., Japan has many volcanoes, which are available for geothermal power generation.	e.g., Suitable construction sites are often located in National Parks.

Step 2 Find a partner and ask your partner about their answers to Step 1, and write them down in the following cards.

Energy source 1 :

✔ **Advantages**   ❌ **Disadvantages**

Energy source 2 :

✔ **Advantages**   ❌ **Disadvantages**

Step 3 Now that you have learned about various renewable energy sources, think of the best combination of renewable energy sources for Japan and write a short essay about it. Explain why it is the best combination, based on the features of each renewable energy source.

Writing Checklist

☐ Clearly stated the best combination of renewable energy sources.

☐ Clearly described the features of the chosen energy sources.

☐ Provided reasonable explanations.

Useful Expressions

• This generates electric power by *how*.

• This is an advantage/disadvantage because *why*.

• They compensate for each other by *how*.

UNIT 3

It's (Not) an Equal World After All

In the 21st century, the UK and other countries have become increasingly ethnically diverse. Today, even in majority white societies, there are many popular figures (such as actors, singers, and athletes) who are ethnic minorities. However, the most influential people in the country are still mostly white.

PHASE 1

1 | Getting into the Topic

Read the following quotes from two of the thousand most influential figures in today's British society. Fill in the blanks with the appropriate words to match the definitions given below. Some letters for each word are given.

Sadiq Khan: London's first Muslim [1](m _ y _ _)
London's greatest strength is our [2](d _ v _ _ s _ _ y), and it's wonderful to see Londoners celebrating our capital's different traditions, determined to stand up to [3](d _ v _ _ _ o n).

Edward Enninful: First black [4](e _ _ _ _ r)-in-chief of British Vogue
My 'Vogue' is about being inclusive; it's about [2](d _ v _ _ s _ _ y). Showing different women, different body shapes, different races, class. To be tackling gender.

Definitions

1. the head of a city, etc.
2. the quality of including a range of many people and things
3. the state of being separated
4. a person who is in charge of managing a magazine, etc.

Advanced

2  1st Viewing

Watch the video and write down the answers to the following questions.

1. The woman shows a list in the opening of the video. What does the list represent?

_____

2. What is the problem with this list?

_____

PHASE 2

1 📋 Vocabulary

Match the words with their definitions.

1. diversity [ ] **a.** to form; to amount to

2. equality [ ] **b.** being at the same level, rank, or status, especially regarding rights and opportunities

3. ethnic [ ]

4. make up [ ] **c.** related to things or people with a shared cultural background

5. establishment [ ] **d.** the quality of including various different types of people or things, especially cultural varieties

6. politically correct [ ]

7. innovative [ ] **e.** the powerful part of society that politically or economically controls or influences the masses; the government

f. being considered appropriate because it does not obviously insult or exclude certain groups of people

g. using original or creative new ways to do something

2 📖 Reading DL 04 CD1-04

Read the following passage.

The Power of Diversity

The world is rapidly changing, and one of the greatest problems for developed countries now is equality. As people move more easily between countries and have more
3   access to education, nations like the United Kingdom (UK) are beginning to worry about

the underrepresentation of ethnic minorities and women. These issues have become so
important that they have even been included in several of the Sustainable Development
Goals (SDGs) set in 2015. Most people would agree that a person's abilities do not depend
on their race or gender. However, in reality, success in society is still not equal.

The largest ethnic group in the UK is white British, and this group makes up about 80%
of the entire population. There is also a much smaller group of non-British white people,
mostly from other European countries. The remaining population of black, Asian, mixed
race, and other ethnic minorities makes up a little less than 15% of the UK population. In
2017, *the Guardian* and Operation Black Vote created a list of the most powerful people
in the country. This list included 1,049 CEOs, government ministers, police and military
personnel, editors, executives, and more. Shockingly, they discovered that less than 40 of
the individuals on the list were non-white. Only 3.4% of the top 1,049 powerful people in
the UK were non-white, and only 0.7% were ethnic minority women. The remaining 96.6%
were white.

Why is this a problem? The people on the list are the most influential people in the
country. They can make laws, hire and fire large numbers of employees, and overall control
the British establishment. Some people believe that this is a problem because if minorities
are not represented in this group of elites, decisions will likely be made from a "white" point
of view. They argue that this is not politically correct and that it can be harmful to minorities,
who do not get a chance to express their opinions. Also, diversity in opinions can help the
UK grow. Studies have shown that diversity can offer competitive advantages to corporations
and institutions. With more people from a wider range of backgrounds in power, more
innovative solutions can be found to the nation's problems. Without proper representation,
ethnic minorities' voices may not be heard, and good potential may be wasted.

The UK has passed laws to promote diversity and equality, but *the Guardian*'s list
suggests that these laws are not enough to bring about large-scale social change. Although
ethnic minorities have been fighting for equality
for a very long time, their fight is still not over.
However, there has been progress, and as the
SDGs help ethnic minorities make their way onto
this list, countries like the UK may become more
diverse and equal.   455 words

Notes

ℓ 12 **Operation Black Vote:** a British nonprofit organization established in 1966 to achieve racial
justice and equality in the UK

3 |  Organizer

Complete the organizer based on the information from the reading.

The Reality of Diversity in British Society

Problem(s)	**What is one of the greatest problems?** [1] _____ [2] _____ are underrepresented in powerful positions.
Details	*How do we know it is a problem?* Proportions of ethnic groups in the UK • White British = about [4] _____ % • [3] _____ = a small proportion • Ethnic minority = less than [5] _____ % Proportions of ethnic groups in the top 1,049 powerful people in the UK • White British/non-British white =[6] _____ % • Non-white =[7] _____ % (➡ Ethnic minority women =[8] _____ %) *Why is it a problem?* • If minorities are not represented in this group of elites, decisions will likely be made from [9] _____ . = Not [10] _____ correct and can be harmful to minorities (Ethnic minorities do not [11] _____ .) • Good potential may be wasted. Studies: Diversity can offer [12] _____ _____ .
Solution	**What is being done about it?** • [13] _____ have been passed. • The SDGs help [14] _____ _____ .

PHASE 3

◼◀ 2nd Viewing

(online / video)

Watch the video again and write down the answers to the following questions.

1. How many people on the list of the most powerful British were not white?

_____

2. Why are Mo Farah, Stormzy, and Idris Elba not on the list?

_____

3. In what professions are there still no non-white leaders? Name at least two.

_____

PHASE 4

💬 ⚡ Output Task (Writing / Speaking)

You have learned that there is inequality in the British establishment. However, this problem does not just exist in the UK. Discuss the possible challenges Asian people face in white-majority societies.

Step I ▶ Think of one influential or important Asian person in white-majority societies and write down some details about them. You may use your own knowledge or do some research.

Name Nationality/Ethnicity	e.g., Michelle Wu, Taiwanese
Occupation	e.g., The mayor of Boston
Reason(s) for being influential/important	e.g., Her bold ideas such as making the city's buses fare-free
Challenge(s) he/she has faced	e.g., Her parents, immigrants from Taiwan, struggled because they could not speak English. As a child, she served as her parents' interpreter.

Advanced

Step 2 Find a partner and introduce the person you wrote about in Step 1 to him/her and discuss the challenges Asian people face in white-majority societies. Also discuss what can be changed to make life and success easier for Asian people in these countries and how these changes can be implemented.

You may ask your partner questions such as:

- What is the name/nationality of the person?
- Why do you think he/she became successful in (*country*)?
- What challenges did he/she face in (*country*)?
- What can the country or individuals do to help Asians succeed in white-majority societies?

Step 3 Based on what you have discussed and learned, do you think there will be more Asian people who thrive in white-majority societies? First, decide on your stance (yes or no) and write why you think so/not with reasons/examples. Then, write a suggestion for making a society that accepts more Asian minorities.

_____

_____

_____

_____

_____

Writing Checklist

☐ Clearly stated his/her main idea.

☐ Gave reasons/explanations/examples for his/her stance.

☐ Gave a clear suggestion for accepting more Asian minorities.

Useful Expressions

- Unfortunately, ...
- In spite of ..., ...
- If I were *who*, then I'd *do what*

Advanced

The Search for a Perfect Partner

UNIT 4

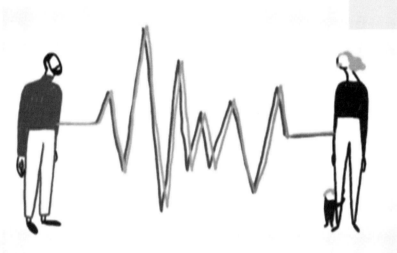

Whether or not you believe in soulmates, most people find themselves, at one point or another, wondering if they will find Miss or Mr. Right. But is that really the question we should be asking? Is the idea of a soulmate optimistic or just lazy?

PHASE 1

1 | Getting into the Topic

Read the following key findings from an annual survey on the attitudes of single people in the US, and fill in the blanks with the appropriate words to match the definitions given below. Some letters for each word are given.

84% want someone they can [1](t _ _ _ t) and confide in

What do single people really want?

84% want someone who can make them laugh

83% want someone open-minded and accepting of [2](d _ _ _ _ r e _ _ _ s)

83% want someone emotionally [3](m _ t _ _ _)

80% want someone who has a life of their own

78% want someone physically [4](a t _ _ _ c _ _ _ _) (vs. 90% in 2020)

Definitions

1. to believe that someone is good, honest, or sincere
2. ways in which two or more people are not the same
3. behaving in a sensible way, like adults
4. pleasing to look at; good-looking

Source: Singles in America 2021

27

2 |  1st Viewing

 online/video

Watch the video and write down the answers to the following questions.

1. What is the only issue the caller has with his new girlfriend?

_____

2. What is Philippa Perry worried that dating has become more like?

_____

PHASE 2

1 | Vocabulary

Match the words with their definitions.

1. **speculate**	[ ]	**a.** to think and form an opinion about something without enough information to be certain
2. **mutual**	[ ]	**b.** shared by two or more people
3. **morph**	[ ]	**c.** suited for one another
4. **compatible**	[ ]	**d.** the power believed to control events; fate
5. **counterproductive**	[ ]	**e.** being a fundamental part of a person, not learned or gained from experience
6. **destiny**	[ ]	**f.** to change in shape or form
7. **hardwired**	[ ]	**g.** against the original intention

2 | Reading

 DL 005   CD1-05

Read the following passage.

The Soulmate Delusion

Many of us look forward to meeting our "soulmate," that is, a romantic partner who is perfect for us. We spend a long time searching for this person, and every time we meet someone new, we agonize about whether we really are destined to be with this person forever.

4 But do soulmates really exist? And if they do, how do we know if he or she is "the one?" Most

⁵ people have speculated about this, both informally and professionally, and almost everyone has developed his or her own opinions on the matter.

When asked for relationship advice by one of her callers, Philippa Perry, agony aunt for *the Guardian*, commented that "no one is quite right for anyone." She explained that relationships take work and that all human beings are "oddly-shaped pieces" that have a ¹⁰ mutual impact upon each other over time. She argued that real attachment only starts when we influence each other and morph together as partners. In a way, although she clearly does not believe in the "soulmate" who comes ready-made in a perfect package, she does believe that people can develop together to become compatible; they go from being two individuals to being one couple.

¹⁵ Although Philippa Perry has not necessarily done research on relationships specifically, some psychologists agree that searching for a ready-made soulmate is actually counterproductive. Dr. C. Raymond Knee, a relationship scientist, describes two different approaches to relationships: "destiny beliefs" and "growth beliefs." People with destiny beliefs believe in the soulmate, and that when they find that person, the relationship will be ²⁰ perfect right away. On the other hand, people with growth beliefs understand that when they meet someone, the relationship will take work and they and their partner will grow together through shared experiences. Research shows that the relationships of people with growth beliefs tend to be more stable and built on a stronger foundation. Because each individual expects differences in opinion or character to arise, they are more prepared to give and take ²⁵ to achieve a healthy balance in the relationship.

In spite of the research and many arguments against the existence of soulmates, human beings seem to be hardwired to search for a perfect partner. This can bring about challenges in romantic relationships, mainly because each party has unreasonable expectations and ends up being disappointed. However, stopping the search for a soulmate should not mean ³⁰ settling for second-best in a relationship. It merely means that any relationship, worthwhile or not, requires effort, and the prospect of problems should not be the deciding factor for ending a relationship. Not all people are compatible, but even those who are compatible are not a match made in ³⁵ heaven. We should all embrace the challenge of *becoming* a perfect pair.

457 words

Notes

ℓ 7   **agony aunt:** a person who works at a newspaper, magazine, or other organization and publishes advice in response to people's emails, letters, or calls discussing their personal problems (also called Dear Abby)

3 |  Organizer

Complete the organizer based on the information from the reading.

Building Successful Relationships

"Soulmate"

Definition: ¹ _____

Philippa Perry (agony aunt)

Beliefs about relationships:

• "No one is ² _____ ."

• Relationships take work.

   ❯ All human beings are "³ _____ " that have a mutual

   ⁴ _____ over time.

• ⁵ _____ only starts when we morph together as partners.

Does she believe in soulmates? ⁶ Yes / No

Research Findings

Two approaches to relationships

Name: ⁷ _____	Name: *growth beliefs*
Description:	Description:
Believes in the soulmate and that when they find that person, the relationship will ⁸ _____	*Understands that the relationship will take work and that they and their partner will* ⁹ _____ _____ _____

Which approach has been found to be more stable? ¹⁰ destiny beliefs / growth beliefs

Why?

• Each individual expects ¹¹ _____ .

   ❯ More prepared to ¹² _____ to achieve a healthy balance in the relationship

PHASE 3

▮◀ 2nd Viewing

(online video)

Watch the video again and write down the answers to the following questions.

1. What does the caller like about his present girlfriend? Give at least two characteristics.

_____

2. According to Philippa Perry, why isn't dating like shopping?

_____

3. According to Philippa Perry, what do we all look for in a partner?

_____

PHASE 4

●●● ↘ Output Task (Writing / Speaking)

Philippa Perry gave some very nice relationship advice to her caller. What kind of advice would you give to someone who wants advice on romance?

Step 1 ▶ Find a partner and read the following two situations. Then, choose one situation each and write advice for the person in that situation.

Derek, 27	Linda, 18
I met my girlfriend in high school and have been dating her for 10 years. I love her very much and we work very well together. Everyone says we should get married, but I'm worried that I have not dated enough people to be sure that she's my soulmate. Should I propose to her or break up with her?	I'm a senior in high school and all my friends have a boyfriend. They want me to get a boyfriend so we can go on double dates. A boy in my class, who I don't really know well, has just broken up with his girlfriend and asked me out. Should I go?

❯ Advice for _____

Step 2 Take turns being Philippa Perry and Derek/Linda. Role play a phone call and do the following.

Flow

1. **Derek/Linda:** Explain the problem your partner chose.

2. **Philippa:** Give Derek/Linda the advice you wrote in Step 1.

3. **Derek/Linda:** Give Philippa feedback on the advice (e.g., Was it helpful? Is it doable? How do you feel now?).

4. Switch roles.

Example (based on the video transcript)

Caller: My new girlfriend is the ideal woman, but she's got a lot of insecurities. I also have a lot of insecurities, so I'm afraid we may not be a good match.

Philippa: First, don't expect a perfect partner because perfect partners don't exist. Also, give your girlfriend reassurance and ask for it, too, because we are all looking for someone with whom we can learn to feel safe.

Caller: Okay, I think I can do that. I'll try encouraging my girlfriend a bit more. Thank you for your thoughtful advice.

Philippa: No problem. Good luck.

Step 3 Use the checklist below to evaluate your partner's counseling and share your comments/feedback with your partner.

Checklist

☐ Your partner clearly considered the issue from your point of view.

☐ Your partner gave concrete advice for your problem.

☐ You found the advice useful.

Comments/Feedback

" "

UNIT 5

Bike Helmets: Are They Safe?

It seems obvious that helmets save cyclists' lives and making helmets compulsory is a good thing. On a grander scale, however, it is not that simple. While it is good for individual cyclists, compulsory helmet-wearing might have a negative impact on the population as a whole.

PHASE 1

1 | Getting into the Topic

The following are the basic rules for riding a bicycle in Japan. Fill in the blanks with the appropriate words from below.

 Five rules to follow to ensure safety when riding a bicycle   Source: National Police Agency

1	In principle, cyclists should ride on the street and use sidewalks only in ¹_____.
2	Cyclists should ride on the left side of the street.
3	Cyclists must reduce speed on sidewalks and give ²_____ the right of way.

4	Cyclists must obey the below safety rules.
	• Do not ride a bicycle — after drinking alcohol.
	             — with two adults on the same bicycle.
	      — ³_____ another cyclist.
	• Use lights at night-time.
	• Follow traffic signals. At ⁴_____, stop and check whether it is safe to cross.

5	Children must wear cycling helmets.

exceptional cases	pedestrians	next to	intersections

2 1st Viewing

Watch the video and write down the answers to the following questions.

1. According to the male narrator in the video, what is the problem when people are discussing their opinions?

_____

2. What is indicated to happen to the amount of cycling if people were forced to wear bike helmets?

_____

PHASE 2

1 Vocabulary

Match the words with their definitions.

1. **recommend**   [   ]   **a.** to say strongly that something is true

2. **assert**   [   ]   **b.** to suggest that something is good to do

3. **aggressive**   [   ]   **c.** something that happens or exists

4. **overreaction**   [   ]   **d.** required to be done by law or a rule

5. **compulsory**   [   ]   **e.** acting angrily and violently

6. **phenomenon**   [   ]   **f.** having awareness of something

7. **conscious**   [   ]   **g.** reaction in an extreme way

2 Reading

 DL 06   CD1-06

Read the following passage.

The Helmet Debate

Cycling regularly is one of the best ways to improve your health and fitness. According to a study of 250,000 commuters conducted by the University of Glasgow, cyclists were half as likely to get cancer and heart disease than non-cyclists. Meanwhile, many cyclists are involved in road accidents, and the number is rising. In Britain, thousands of cyclists each year are
5 seriously injured on the roads, leading experts to strongly recommend that cyclists wear a

helmet.

However, opinions on cycle helmets are divided in Britain. Dr. John Black, a doctor of emergency medicine, believes that cycling helmets should be made mandatory. He has seen first-hand the damage that results from not wearing a helmet, from life-changing head injuries to deaths. He asserts that simply making helmets obligatory would save many lives. On the other hand, some believe that helmet-wearing should be down to personal choice. "If you want to wear a helmet, wear a helmet," says cyclist Chris Boardman, a former professional racing cyclist and British Olympic gold medalist. Nick Hussey, founder of cycling goods brand Vulpine, agrees with this. He argues that cycling is often associated with danger, which in turn discourages many people from taking up the activity. The need to wear a helmet is not viewed as a precaution, but a symbol of the need to protect one's head (a vital part of the body) from injury. He complains that whenever he releases marketing photos using models without helmets, he receives a large number of aggressive comments criticizing cycling without a helmet, which he thinks is an overreaction.

This leads us to wonder if making helmets compulsory really works. In New Zealand, the number of bike trips halved almost immediately after a law enforcing the use of helmets was introduced in 1994. The same phenomenon occurred in Sydney, Australia. Public health officials believe that reversing that decision would actually save more lives because people would cycle more and improve their health. Some suggest that rather than making people wear helmets, creating a safer environment for cyclists is more important. In the Netherlands, where over 27% of all trips are made by bicycle, people are highly conscious of road safety. Traffic lessons start in school at age five, and as children grow older, they all begin cycling to school. Although there is no campaign to make cycle helmets compulsory in the Netherlands, cycling has become safer over time as a result of the widespread cycling culture.

The Guardian investigations revealed that the health benefits of cycling far outweigh the risks associated with cycling without a helmet. What we should really fear are the negative impacts of an inactive lifestyle on public health. As both those in support of and against compulsory helmet-wearing have compelling arguments, perhaps it is time to consider a compromise, rather than trying to choose a side.

472 words

Notes

ℓ 7 **Dr. John Black:** a medical director at the South Central Ambulance Service NHS Foundation Trust (SCAS) in the UK

ℓ 12 **Chris Boardman:** gold medalist in the 1992 Barcelona Olympics, who brought the first gold medal to Britain in 72 years. He became a professional cyclist in 1993.

3 | 📄 Organizer

Complete the organizer based on the information from the reading.

🚲 Cycling

Benefits	Disadvantages
• One of the best ways to [1] _____ _____ .	• Cyclists are often involved in [3] _____ _____ .
Example: Cyclists were [2] _____ _____ than non-cyclists.	**Example in Britain:** [4] _____ each year are seriously injured.

⛑ Divided Opinions on Compulsory Helmet-Wearing

For	Against
Dr. John Black believes [5] _____ _____ because simply making helmets obligatory [6] _____ _____ .	**Chris Boardman believes** "[7] _____ _____ ." **Nick Hussey believes** cycling is often associated with danger. ➤ It discourages many people from [8] _____ _____ **After compulsory helmet wearing was enforced by law in New Zealand (1994),** [9] _____ _____ .

🚶🚲 Creating a Safer Environment for Cyclists

The Netherlands:

- Over 27% of all trips are made by bicycle.
- People are highly conscious of [10] _____ .
- Traffic lessons start in school at [11] _____ .
- There is no campaign to make cycle helmets compulsory in the Netherlands, but cycling is becoming safer [12] _____ because of cycling culture.

PHASE 3

◾◀ 2nd Viewing

Watch the video again and write down the answers to the following questions.

1. What is the benefit of cycling to people's health?

_____

2. What does "risk compensation" mean?

_____

3. What things did the Dutch do to make cycling safer in the Netherlands? Give at least one.

_____

PHASE 4

💬✏️ Output Task (Writing / Speaking)

Attention to safe cycling has been growing. Some people believe that wearing a helmet is the answer, while others argue that bike-friendly infrastructures are the key. What do you think can make cycling safer in your community?

Step 1 ▶ Imagine you are a city councilor for your city. Add one idea to make cycling safer in your city. Then, write down a plan for each idea.

Ideas to make cycling safer

Ideas	How to do this
Promote helmet use	(Your plan) e.g., Making a poster to explain that wearing a bike helmet can save lives
Another idea _____ e.g., Making roads safer	(Your plan) e.g., Building more bicycle-only lanes

Step 2 ▶ Share your ideas for safer cycling with some classmates. Write down which plan you think is most effective and why.

Most Effective Plan:

→ *Reasons it is most effective:*

_____

_____

Step 3 ▶ Imagine you are making a speech at the city council. Try to convince the other councilors to implement your plan. Use the following structure to make your speech logical.

In order to make cycling safer in our city, we should _____

_____.

Here are _____ reasons.

First, _____.

Second, _____.

⋮ (optional) Add more reasons.

In conclusion, _____.

Presentation Checklist

☐ The plan is clearly explained.

☐ Convincing reasons are provided for the plan.

☐ Strategies (body language, eye contact, etc.) are used to grab the audience's attention.

Green Fabrics: Toward a Sustainable Fashion Industry

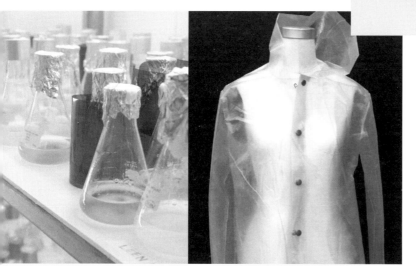

In the 21st century, mass-produced cheap clothing has become a problem. In response, scientists have been working on developing new fabrics for more sustainable fashion. Algae, a type of plant, is one source of these newly developing eco-friendly "green" fabrics.

PHASE 1

1 | Getting into the Topic

Based on the two infographics about the environmental impacts of clothing, choose T (True) or F (False) for each sentence. (These infographics use UK spelling.)

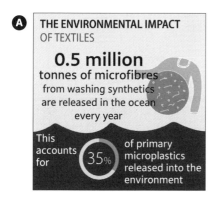

A THE ENVIRONMENTAL IMPACT OF TEXTILES

0.5 million tonnes of microfibres from washing synthetics are released in the ocean every year

This accounts for **35%** of primary microplastics released into the environment

B THE ENVIRONMENTAL IMPACT OF TEXTILES

10% of global greenhouse gas emissions are caused by clothing and footwear production

This is more than all international flights and maritime shipping combined

Source: European Parliamentary Research Service

1. Infographic **A** shows the impact in the production process of clothing.　　　　　[T / F]

2. Infographic **A** suggests that the type of material used for clothes can have a serious impact on the environment.　　　　　[T / F]

3. Infographic **B** shows that the airline industry is not responsible for environmental degradation.　　　　　[T / F]

2 ◼◀ 1st Viewing

Watch the video and write down the answers to the following questions.

1. What is the green substance in the lab scenes?

_____

2. What is the presentation by Charlotte McCurdy (designer and researcher) about?

_____

PHASE 2

1 📋 Vocabulary

Match the words with their definitions.

1. **fashion fabric** [ ]   **a.** a type of fabric for creating clothing that meets the latest fashion trends

2. **synthetic** [ ]

3. **textile** [ ]   **b.** any type of cloth made by hand or machine

4. **barometer** [ ]   **c.** able to naturally break down without harming the environment

5. **biodegradable** [ ]   **d.** an area where waste is buried under the earth

6. **landfill** [ ]   **e.** able to take more CO_2 out of the air than is produced

7. **carbon-negative** [ ]   **f.** produced by combining different chemical substances

    g. a way to measure the changes in something, such as people's opinions

2 📖 Reading

 DL 07   ◉ CD1-07

Read the following passage.

The Rise of Green Fashion

Clothes are one of the most basic parts of human life. But what are they made of? Cotton has been used in clothing for centuries and is made from naturally grown cotton plants. Another common fashion fabric, polyester, is a synthetic plastic fiber that is usually made

4 from petroleum. It became highly popular after World War II. According to Dr. Mark Liu,

a fashion and textile designer, "materials have evolved with culture and society and are a barometer of the technology we have at the time." So, what do our modern materials say about society today?

Although cotton and polyester are the two most commonly used materials for clothing, the new "fast fashion" trend has sparked a debate about whether they are good fabrics to use. From an environmental perspective, both are unsustainable. The plastics in polyester clothes are not biodegradable and contain large amounts of carbon. According to Charlotte McCurdy, fabrics like polyester that are made from fossil fuels emit carbon-dioxide (CO_2) during the production process. Meanwhile, cotton is natural, but takes a lot of time, energy, and resources to grow and make into clothes. Since "fast fashion" produces massive quantities of very cheap clothing at low prices, it requires larger amounts of fabric than ever before. Also, although so much clothing is being produced, people buy it and quickly throw it away. Many of the clothes are going to landfills and the ones that contain polyester are sitting there for years because they are not biodegradable.

The fashion industry's impact on the environment has pushed researchers to explore and develop new and more sustainable fabrics. Dr. Mark Liu and Charlotte McCurdy are just two researchers who are making fabrics with different kinds of algae, which are a type of plant usually found in water. Dr. Liu uses microalgae (very small algae that you cannot see) and McCurdy uses macroalgae (larger visible algae, like seaweed). Dr. Liu's microalgae fabrics are eco-friendly because, unlike cotton, they do not require a lot of space, water, or human labor and they can grow very quickly. Meanwhile, McCurdy's macroalgae raincoat is carbon-negative because, unlike polyester, it is made from plants that are currently consuming CO_2 and releasing oxygen into the air. Both researchers have used science to develop solutions to the problems that cotton and polyester cause in fast fashion.

While researchers work to develop new fabrics, fashion and textile companies are already making clothes from new sustainable biodegradable materials. Bolt Threads, for example, has created an imitation spider silk by studying silk made from real spiders and using science to mass-produce it in yeast! They collaborated with Stella McCartney and MOMA to create a spider silk gold dress that was shown in New York in 2017. The future of fashion is not just in the design: it is in the material! 469 words

Eco-leather bags on display

Advanced

3 | 📄 Organizer

Complete the organizer based on the information from the reading.

Fashion Fabrics: Past and Present

Kind	Polyester fabrics	Cotton fabrics	Algae fabrics
Production *(source/origin, resources used, etc.)*	*A synthetic plastic fiber usually made from* 1 _____	*Made from* 2 _____	2 Types of Algae: • 3 _____ • 4 _____
History *(introduction, popularity, etc.)*	*Became highly* 5 _____ after 6 _____	*Used for* 7 _____	*Introduced by* • Dr. Mark Liu • 8 _____
Features *(good and bad)*	Pros: Quick, easy, and cheap to produce Cons: • Emits CO_2 • Not 9 _____	Cons: • Takes 10 _____ _____ to grow and make into clothes	Pros: Microalgae Don't require 11 _____ _____ ➡ Can grow very quickly Macroalgae Carbon negative ➡ Made from plants that are 12 _____ _____
Result *(environmental effects)*	Unsustainable (goes to landfills)	Unsustainable (emits 13 _____ _____)	14 _____

PHASE 3

◼◀ 2nd Viewing

online video

Watch the video again and write down the answers to the following questions.

1. Why is polyester bad for the environment?

_____

2. Why does Dr. Liu compare the production process of microalgae with that of cotton?

_____

3. Besides the algae fabrics, what sustainable fabrics are mentioned at the end of the video?

_____

PHASE 4

💬✍ Output Task (Writing / Speaking)

Do you think sustainable fabrics such as algae will replace cotton and polyester fabrics?

Step 1 Fill in the table below with the pros and cons of one sustainable fabric and one traditional fabric of your choice from the perspectives of cost, durability, impacts on the environment, etc.

	Pros	Cons
Sustainable fabric ( )		
Traditional fabric ( )		

Step 2 Find a partner and role play a conversation between a shop clerk and a customer. The shop clerk wants to sell sustainable fabric items, but the customer is not so sure about them.

⊙ Be sure that the clerk explains good points of sustainable fabrics, while the customer expresses concerns about them.

You may use expressions like such as:

Clerk	
	You can contribute to the fight against global warming by _____.
	You'll be proud to wear it because _____.
	I'm sure you'll like it because _____.
	It's true that it costs a bit of extra, but _____.

Customer	
	What about durability? Doesn't it fray quickly?
	Is it washable? Doesn't it get torn easily?
	Isn't it a little expensive?

Step 3 Now that you have understood the pros and cons of sustainable fabrics, do you think sustainable fabrics will replace traditional fabrics? First, decide on your stance (yes or no). Then, write a suggestion for how to proceed with future fashion fabrics.

If you choose **"yes"**	❱ Write one suggestion for how to promote sustainable fabrics to young people.
If you choose **"no"**	❱ Write one suggestion for how the fashion industry should address environmental issues while continuing to use traditional fabrics.

_____

_____

_____

_____

_____

✎ Writing Checklist

☐ Clarified his/her stance on the given theme.

☐ Gave a clear suggestion for the future fashion fabric industry.

☐ Gave a concluding remark to verify his/her claim.

Useful Expressions

• I suggest *who do what*.
• This is effective because …
• This can help *who* by *how*.
• In sum/conclusion, …

How Does Water Taste?
Ask a Water Sommelier

Seventy-one percent of the Earth's surface is covered with water, famously one of the main reasons the planet is full of life. But in spite of its abundance, water on this planet is precious … and delicious. While people often take water for granted and even dare to call it "boring," it is both a necessity and a luxury.

PHASE 1

1 | Getting into the Topic

Read about five common types of water, and fill in the blanks with the appropriate words from below. The first one is done for you.

spring water	Water that comes directly from underground sources
[1]( ) **water**	Water that comes directly from a named underground source. It must be bottled directly at the source.
[2]( ) **water**	Water that is carbonated and sometimes includes minerals, also called fizzy water
[3]( ) **water**	Water that has been filtered or processed to remove impurities like chemicals and other contaminants
[4]( ) **water**	Water that comes directly from the faucet of your home or office

purified	sparkling	mineral	tap

2 | 1st Viewing

online video

Watch the video and write down the answers to the following questions.

1. How much does 9OH2O cost?

_____

2. What are Martin Riese and the interviewer doing in the video?

_____

PHASE 2

1 | Vocabulary

Match the words with their definitions.

1. **appreciate**   [   ]   **a.** to see and approve something's value

2. **texture**   [   ]   **b.** to draw attention to an important point

3. **mineral**   [   ]   **c.** something found naturally in the Earth, but that is not living; for example, salt

4. **note**   [   ]   **d.** having a relaxing quality that helps to restore someone's health

5. **therapeutic**   [   ]   **e.** to make someone else believe what you believe without forcing them to do so

6. **convince**   [   ]   **f.** having been passed through a material that takes out unwanted substances

7. **filtered**   [   ]   **g.** the feeling something has when you touch it; for example, smooth or rough

2 | Reading

 DL 08   CD1-08

Read the following passage.

A Mission to Make People Appreciate Water

What would you say is the planet's most precious resource? Some would say gold or platinum or other precious metals and gems. Ask German-born water sommelier, Martin Riese, however, and he would say water. Our very existence relies on the availability of clean
4   drinking water, and Riese is on a mission to get people to appreciate water's value.

The word "sommelier" is a French word usually associated with waiters at fancy restaurants who specialize in wine. However, Riese is an expert in the taste and quality of different types of water. Since discovering the different tastes of water at age five while traveling around Europe with his family, Riese has loved tasting various different types of water. Some may laugh at the idea of water-tasting, but Riese explains that each type of water has a completely different taste and texture depending on its source. Most people have probably heard of the various types of water, such as "natural mineral water," "spring water," or "table water," but many do not know the actual differences between them.

According to Riese, minerals are key when selecting water for your taste. He explains that if you do not like the taste of a certain water, it is likely due to the mineral content. He recommends trying many different waters to find one that fits you. To help people with this, Riese offers his services as a water sommelier, giving people advice and suggestions on how to drink water. After moving to the US, he created a water menu at a restaurant in Los Angeles, which includes 20 types of water, and he offers water-tasting events at $50 per person!

Riese also notes that water is not and should not be "pure." In its natural state, water is packed with minerals, and Europeans have embraced this concept throughout history, using mineral water for both drinking and bathing. In Europe, naturally sourced water has been loved for its healing and therapeutic qualities. However, in the US, some people have become overly fearful of germs and bacteria, so companies have created bottled mineral water that is mainly purified tap water with minerals added later. These waters are highly processed and not sustainably sourced. Riese hopes to convince Americans that tap water filtered at home is much better for both people and the planet.

Most living things cannot survive without water. However, water is not only a necessity, but also a luxury. Martin Riese and other water sommeliers around the world are trying to educate people, especially in developed countries, about the value and art of water. These sommeliers hold water-tasting events and advise both consumers and companies on how to make the water-drinking experience most enjoyable.   449 words

---

Notes

ℓ 23 **germ:** a small living thing, usually one that causes disease or infections

ℓ 23 **bacteria:** the simplest and smallest forms of life; a type of germ that exists in both living and dead creatures, and that is often a cause of disease

3 |  Organizer

Complete the organizer based on the information from the reading.

About Martin Riese

Occupation	**Water sommelier** = an expert in [1] _____ _____ Martin Riese created [2] _____ at a restaurant in LA. ┌─────────────────┐ │ What does he do? │ └─────────────────┘ • He gives people advice and suggestions on [3] _____ _____ . • He offers [4] _____ at $50 per person.
Nationality	[5] _____
Inspiration	[6] _____ while traveling around Europe when he was 5 years old
Belief(s) & Argument(s)	• Water is the planet's most precious resource. • Each type of water has a completely different [7] _____ and [8] _____ depending on [9] _____ . • [10] _____ are key when selecting water for your taste. • Water is not and should not be "[11] _____ ." • [12] _____ filtered at home is much better than bottled water for both people and the planet. • Water is not only [13] _____ , but also [14] _____ .
Advice	• Try many different waters to find one that fits you • Drink tap water filtered at home
Goal	Educate people about [15] _____

PHASE 3

🎞◀ 2nd Viewing

(online / video)

Watch the video again and write down the answers to the following questions.

1. Why did Riese swirl his glass before drinking the water?

_____

2. What "magic trick" did Riese play on the Danish water?

_____

3. How did Riese describe Vichy Catalan? Give at least one piece of information.

_____

PHASE 4

💬✎ Output Task (Writing / Speaking)

You knew about wine sommeliers, and now you know about water sommeliers. Now it's your turn! Become a something sommelier and teach us about something you love.

Step 1 ▶ Choose ONE drink or food that has many types or brands (you can choose chocolate, tea, or other). For the food/drink you chose, list some features for each of the different types/brands.

Item	Types/Brands	Features
Example: Water 🍷	1. Fiji 2. 9OH2O 3. Vichy Catalan	1. neutral, not much flavor 2. smooth, like olive oil, round texture 3. strong, salty, Spanish
Chocolate 🍫	1. Dark 2. White 3. Milk 4. Ruby	1. 2. 3. 4.
Tea ☕	1. Straight black tea 2. Tea with lemon 3. Tea with milk	1. 2. 3.
Other _____	1. 2. 3.	1. 2. 3.

Advanced

Step 2 Find a partner and role play a mock tasting session.

Flow

1. **Sommelier:** List different types/brands of something.

2. **Guest:** Ask question(s).

3. **Sommelier:** Give detailed explanations about each type/brand.

4. **Guest:** Tell the sommelier which one you choose and why.

5. Switch roles.

Example (based on the video transcript)

Sommelier: Today, I would like to introduce you to three brands of water: Fiji, 9OH2O, and Vichy Catalan.

Guest: Great. Which one will we try first?

Sommelier: Here is Fiji. It's a very neutral water. It doesn't have much flavor. Next, here is 9OH2O. It's round and smooth. And finally, here is Vichy Catalan. It's a Spanish water. It's very strong and salty.

Guest: Thank you. I like Vichy Catalan the most because I like strong drinks.

Step 3 After the tasting session, fill in the following evaluation card.

Rate your experience from 1–5.	☆ ☆ ☆ ☆ ☆
Which brand/type was your favorite? Why?	
Which brand/type did you least like? Why?	
Would you recommend the food/drink to someone else? ❯ If so, why and to whom? ❯ If not, why not?	

UNIT 8
Emerging Forms of Family

Everyone is born from a mother and a father, but the idea of "family" is different for every person. Some people have both of their parents, while others have only one. Some people are adopted or raised by grandparents. Some people are very close to their parents, while others may never speak to them. Amid all of this variety, what can we say is a "mom?"

PHASE 1

1 | Getting into the Topic

Read the following excerpt from an online discussion board and put the underlined words into the correct form.

My mom is a toxic parent. She judges everything I do!

She's so narcissistic and [1] **judgment**—the other day she said my boyfriend must be a playboy.

I can't tolerate her anymore...what should I do?

💬 ⤴ ♡

✎ 2 answers

Ask her to stop!!

How about you stop needing her?
[2] **Easy** said than done, but don't tell her any more about your life.

You may sometimes miss your mother, though. If that's the case, I know a good service that provides you "[3] **mother** advice" from someone other than your [4] **biology** mother...

1._____   2._____   3._____   4._____

2 | ◼◀ 1st Viewing

Watch the video and write down the answers to the following questions.

1. Where are the man and the woman talking at the beginning and end of the video?

_____

2. Who is giving advice in the video?

_____

PHASE 2

1 | 📋 Vocabulary

Match the words with their definitions.

1. viewpoint	[ ]	**a.** the features of a living thing that are passed on by DNA
2. genetics	[ ]	**b.** the action or fact of legally taking another person's child and bringing him/her up as one's own
3. adoption	[ ]	
4. biological	[ ]	**c.** a person's opinion or perspective
5. challenge	[ ]	**d.** related by blood
6. temporarily	[ ]	**e.** a feeling of friendship
7. companionship	[ ]	**f.** to say or do something questioning the truth or validity of something else
		g. for a limited period of time; not permanently

2 | 📖 Reading

🎧 DL 09   ⊙ CD2-02

Read the following passage.

The 21st Century Family

The word "family" has always meant different things for different people. In the 21st century, however, people have begun to express these different viewpoints. The traditional family consisted of people related by blood or genetics who lived together until the children

4 became adults. Although adoption has existed for a long time and same-sex marriage has

been legal in many places, people have often thought of family as a legally married mother and father and their biological children. Recently, however, novels and films have also challenged this idea: *Shoplifters*, directed by Hirokazu Kore-eda, shows a group of people who are not related, but each plays a role as part of a family. Nina Keneally, an experienced mother who lives in New York, also challenges this traditional idea with her service, NeedaMom.

Nina Keneally has been a mother for over 30 years. When she moved to New York City, she noticed that many young people in her neighborhood had no one to talk to about their problems. She decided, for a small fee, to temporarily become their mother and listen to their troubles. With her NeedaMom service, Keneally gives her "children" advice based on her life experiences, providing a warm and caring environment just like a perfect mother would. Her main selling point is that she provides a non-judgment zone, which many of her clients unfortunately do not get from their biological parents. She is not a professional therapist, but simply a loving and experienced mother who enjoys helping young people with their problems.

Recently, more people are beginning to offer similar "family" services. In Japan, rent-a-family services exist to allow lonely people to experience having a family or romantic partner. Although rental family members do not live with and are not genetically related to their clients, they temporarily play the part of a husband, wife or child. Clients can choose different "actors" each time and pay for these "family" services. In exchange, the client can spend time talking, eating meals and going out to play in the park with their "family" just like traditional families do. Although some people think this is odd and unhealthy, it has helped lonely people or people with difficulties socializing. Thanks to the Internet, people who want help or companionship can easily find and use these services.

Nina Keneally and others like her provide company and support to people who have become isolated, thereby helping local communities and fostering healthier relationships among people. Their services may be unconventional, but as the times change, so do people's needs. It seems that rather than seeking professional help from doctors and therapists, people are beginning to turn to complete strangers for advice and comfort. Although they are not biologically related, who is to say they are not "family?"   459 words

3 | 📄 Organizer

Complete the organizer based on the information from the reading.

Emerging Types of Family

🏠 Traditional family

- Related by [1]_____ or [2]_____
- Live together
- A legally [3]_____

🏠 21st century "family"

Type 1 **"NeedaMom" service**

Who is Nina Keneally?

- Mother with [4]_____ years of experience
- Not a [5]_____

What does she do?

- Listens to her "children's" troubles and gives advice for [6]_____
- Provides a [7]_____
- Provides a [8]_____ zone

Type 2 **Rent-a-family services**

Purpose: to allow [9]_____
_____

Similarities to traditional family:

- There are a husband/wife and child(ren)
- Spend time [10]_____
_____
_____

Differences from traditional family:

- Do not live with and are not [11]_____
_____ to their clients
- Are "[12]_____" (who play the part of a family member) that can be chosen
- Temporary
- Paid

PHASE 3

◼◀ 2nd Viewing

(online video)

Watch the video again and write down the answers to the following questions.

1. What did Nina Keneally notice about her neighborhood that made her start her NeedaMom service?

_____

2. Give one example of a problem about which Keneally has been asked for advice.

_____

3. According to Keneally, what does a "good mother" offer?

_____

PHASE 4

💬✓ Output Task (Writing / Speaking)

Nina Keneally provides young people in her neighborhood with a safe place to get motherly advice. Another place people often anonymously ask for help is in Dear Abby letters in newspapers and magazines. Write a Dear Abby letter and a response.

Step I ▶ Think of a problem you are currently facing. Write it down and give up to three reasons why it is troubling you. This can be a problem at school, at home, at work, or anywhere else.

Example

> **The Problem:** There is a girl at work, but I don't know how to woo her.
> **Reasons:**
> • I only see her at work.
> • I wrote a letter, but I want to be more than pen pals.
> • I am too shy to ask her on a date.

The Problem	
Reasons	1.
	2.
	3.

Advanced

Step 2 ▶ Read the brief explanation and samples of "Dear Abby" letter and write a Dear Abby letter asking for advice about your problem. Then, find a partner and switch letters. Write a response to their letter.

What is a "Dear Abby" letter?

A "Dear Abby" letter is a letter asking for advice. It is usually short and includes some background information followed by a question. It is usually signed with a pen name, not the writer's real name. The first word of the pen name is usually used in the response.

Example

> Dear Abby,
> There is a girl at work who I am trying to woo. I wrote her a letter, but I want to be more than pen pals. What should I do next?
> Lonely Heart

> Dear Lonely,
> Writing a letter is romantic, but you need to meet her to woo her. Ask her out for a casual drink and see if she really is a good fit for you.
> Abby

Your Problem

Dear Abby,

Your Partner's Response

Dear

Step 3 ▶ Use the checklist below to evaluate your partner's response and share your comments/feedback with your partner.

Checklist

- ☐ Your partner understood your problem well.
- ☐ Your partner gave concrete advice on your problem.
- ☐ You found the advice useful.

Comments/Feedback

The Dark Side of Robots with Common Sense

AI technology is making robots smarter, possibly even smarter than humans. What should smart robots be like in the future? Do they *need* to be intelligent like humans, or should they be intelligent in a different way? Should these clever robots be expected to act ethically like humans? Are they going to be our friends or our enemies?

PHASE 1

1 | Getting into the Topic

Read the following statements about the humanoid AI robot Sophia, and guess T (True) or F (False) for each statement.

1 Sophia was created by a female scientist. [T / F]

2 Sophia was granted citizenship in Saudi Arabia. [T / F]

3 Sophia once said she would destroy humankind. [T / F]

4 Sophia has a Ph.D. in biology. [T / F]

5 During an interview, Sophia expressed her desire to have a baby. [T / F]

6 Although Sophia communicates well with humans, she is not capable of displaying humanlike expressions. [T / F]

Advanced

2  1st Viewing

online video

Watch the video and write down the answers to the following questions.

1. According to Professor Seth, in what way are computers already cleverer than humans?

_____

2. What is the big challenge for AI now?

_____

PHASE 2

1 📋 Vocabulary

Match the words with their definitions.

1. outperform [   ]   **a.** using physical force to injure or kill someone

2. ethically [   ]   **b.** to do something in exactly the same way

3. evaluate [   ]   **c.** in a right way based on morals

4. inhibit [   ]   **d.** to be better than someone else at doing something

5. aggressively [   ]   **e.** angrily and threateningly

6. violent [   ]   **f.** to judge the value of something

7. replicate [   ]   **g.** to stop or restrain something

2 📖 Reading

 DL 10   CD2-03

Read the following passage.

Will Ethical Robots Breed Unethical Robots?

As artificial intelligence (AI) becomes widespread in society, it is playing a far bigger role than anyone had ever imagined. For example, Google's search algorithms use AI to produce individually targeted advertising. In addition, AI is used by corporations during staff recruitment to decide which candidates to invite for interviews. Now that AI is capable

⁵ of doing work like this, many people wonder whether machines will eventually become more intelligent than humans.

The answer to this depends on how you define "intelligence." Machines already outperform humans not only in highly complex calculations, but also in detecting patterns from large volumes of data. However, according to Professors Anil Seth and Alan Winfield, ¹⁰ there are two things humans are far better at: predicting the future and behaving ethically. Seth, who specializes in cognitive and computational neuroscience, explains that what is core to human intelligence is the ability to perceive the world and make decisions with common sense. For example, if you are walking down the street and see a hole in the ground and someone is about to fall into that hole, it is common sense to try to warn them. It is difficult ¹⁵ for robots to make decisions like this.

In one of his experiments, robotics expert Winfield developed special robots that behaved in a very simple, ethical way. These robots were programmed to evaluate the consequences of each possible action they could take. Any action that had a "bad" consequence for the robot or its surrounding environment was to be inhibited. However, scientists are also uncertain ²⁰ about the safety of developing ethical robots. In an experiment conducted by Winfield's colleague, Dieter Vanderelst, robots began by helping each other, but after their logic was subtly altered, they started to behave aggressively toward each other. This suggests that with only a bit of reprogramming, a robot with ethical decision-making capabilities can easily be transformed into a violent one.

²⁵ Winfield worries that, for example, using this technology, manufacturers could develop robots that behave unethically for their own financial gain. Or, in the worst cases, ethics settings for driverless cars could be vulnerable to malicious hacking. Technical governance, such as placing ethical rules behind strong encryption, is thus vital in order to lessen such risks. Even by taking such measures, however, we cannot rely on machines such as cars, which ³⁰ have the potential to kill humans, to be controlled by ethical robots.

Seth states that the point of AI is not to completely replicate human ability. The fact is, as evidenced through the many tragic events in human history, we do not always act in a moral or rational manner. As he tells us, it is vital that humans continue to think about ³⁵ how to effectively and safely coexist with AI in the future.   460 words

Notes

ℓ 28 **encryption:** the act of putting information into a special code, especially in order to prevent people from looking at it without authority

3 📄 Organizer

Complete the organizer based on the information from the reading.

AI in Society

Who	When	For what purpose
Google's search algorithms	—	to produce individually targeted advertising
Corporations	during 1 _____ _____	2 _____ _____

Many people wonder whether machines will eventually become more intelligent than humans.

What Intelligence Means

Human Intelligence

Humans are far better at	Human intelligence = the ability to
• 3 _____ • 4 _____	• perceive the world • 5 _____

Ethical Robots

Scientist are uncertain about 6 _____.

Vanderelst's robots:

First, they were 7 _____.

After their logic was subtly altered, they started to 8 _____.

AI in the Future

• The point of AI is not 9 _____.

• It is vital that humans continue to think about 10 _____

_____.

PHASE 3

◼◀ 2nd Viewing

(online / video)

Watch the video again and write down the answers to the following questions.

1. What is special and unusual about Professor Winfield's robots in the video?

_____

2. Why does Professor Seth say "the question is how much inspiration we should take from human behavior?"

_____

_____

3. If machines are conscious, what will probably happen to humans and machines?

_____

PHASE 4

💬✎ Output Task (Writing / Speaking)

You have learned that AI technology may enable robots to make ethical decisions. However, making such decisions can be very difficult. Is it really a good idea to leave such decisions to robots? Think about how an ethical robot should behave in the following situation.

Step 1 ▶ Imagine the following situation, then answer the following question.

> **Situation**
> You have told an ethical AI robot to guard your watermelon field. A hungry man tries to steal a watermelon from the field. The man tells the robot that, without the watermelon, he will starve to death. What do you think the robot should do?

Question Write down all possible choices.

e.g., The robot should protect the watermelon field and stop the man from stealing the watermelon.

- _____
- _____
- _____

Step 2 Find a partner and discuss the possible behaviors an ethical robot could take in the situation given in Step 1. List them in the order of appropriateness. In addition, write down reasons why using ethical robots could be good or bad.

Possible behaviors an ethical robot could take

1. _____ Very appropriate

2. _____

3. _____

4. _____ Not so appropriate

✔ **Good**

❌ **Bad**

Step 3 Imagine you are the owner of the watermelon field and considering putting a new robot on your field. Do you want to use an ethical robot or a traditional one? Decide on your stance with reasons. Then, describe the robot in terms of its behavior (e.g., what tasks it engages in, what decisions it makes, etc.).

_____

_____

_____

_____

_____

✏ **Writing Checklist**

☐ Clearly stated his/her position in whether to use an ethical robot or not.

☐ Gave reasons to support his/her position.

☐ Explained logically using signal words.

Useful Expressions

• It should/should not *do what* because ...

• The priority should be ...

• On the one hand, ... On the other hand, ...

Mission to Make Space Exploration Sustainable

Surprisingly to most people, the space around our planet is now crowded with pieces of debris, or space junk. Such junk is a problem because it can cause damage to satellites orbiting around the Earth, which are now an indispensable part of our daily lives. Who can clean up this mess and how?

PHASE 1

1 Getting into the Topic

The following are common applications of artificial satellites. Fill in the blanks with the appropriate words from below.

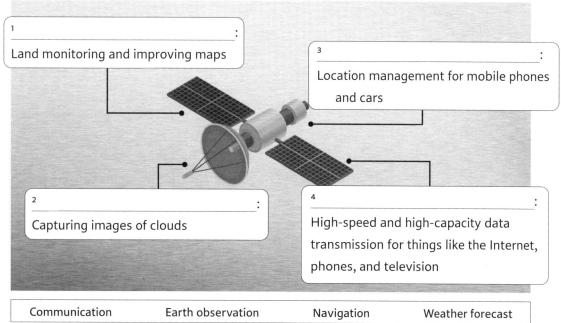

1 _____ :
Land monitoring and improving maps

3 _____ :
Location management for mobile phones and cars

2 _____ :
Capturing images of clouds

4 _____ :
High-speed and high-capacity data transmission for things like the Internet, phones, and television

| Communication | Earth observation | Navigation | Weather forecast |

2 |  1st Viewing

Watch the video and write down the answers to the following questions.

1. What do the orange dots represent in the opening scene?

_____

2. What are some examples of how satellites are used? Give at least three.

_____

PHASE 2

1 | Vocabulary

Match the words with their definitions.

1. orbit   [   ]   **a.** the state of living for a long time

2. debris   [   ]   **b.** to make a situation less serious

3. collide   [   ]   **c.** to run into each other

4. urgent   [   ]   **d.** something broken into pieces

5. mitigate   [   ]   **e.** having no way of leaving from a place

6. stranded   [   ]   **f.** to go around the Earth or other planets

7. longevity   [   ]   **g.** needing to be done right away

2 | 📖 Reading   🎧 DL 11   💿 CD2-04

Read the following passage.

Securing Space Sustainability

Orbiting the Earth at high speed are millions of pieces of man-made debris known as "space junk." Over 90% of this debris has accumulated over only 60 years of human space exploration. It comprises anything from shards of paint and screws to large chunks off of
4   spacecraft and even whole satellites! Because this junk orbits the Earth at around 8 km per

second, it causes immense damage when it collides with satellites or spacecraft, not only costing us a fortune and potentially inconveniencing us, but also introducing even more junk.

As of 2020, there were nearly 6,000 artificial satellites orbiting the Earth, over 2,600 of which were actually operational. These numbers present not only a moral issue with mankind polluting outer space, but also a practical issue that affects human life. On the one hand, many of these satellites are used for communication, such as providing people with television, radio, and the Internet. We rely on them for our weather forecasting and even banking! Although many people take the Internet for granted, it is thanks to the many satellites up in space that we can access the Web almost anywhere on the Earth. On the other hand, however, the increase in satellites in orbit will exponentially increase the potential for collisions, which would create even more debris and then more collisions, a dangerous cascading effect known as Kessler syndrome. Experts argue the urgent need for proper management of the junk, but who should be responsible for cleaning up?

Japanese entrepreneur, Mitsunobu Okada, was the first person to tackle this problem head on. Deeply inspired by NASA astronaut Mamoru Mohri, Okada pursued his passion for space, and in 2013, he founded Astroscale, the first private company to tackle sustainability in space. However, it turned out that the space junk problem had become more serious than he had first imagined. Attending an international conference about space junk, Okada learned that no one was able to offer concrete solutions to the problem. Determined to solve this problem, he traveled the world, pitching his ideas to scientists and engineers. Finally, in 2021, his team at Astroscale succeeded in capturing its first piece of space junk with its demonstration satellite.

Although there are guidelines to mitigate space clutter, such as the UN's request for all satellites to be removed from space after 25 years, the reality is that most satellites are left stranded and discarded. Recently, experts have shifted their focus from the removal of space junk to improving satellite maintenance and advancing technology to increase the lifespan of new satellites. The goal now seems to be simply to try not to make more junk than necessary. Okada, however, has set himself a target to remove all space debris by 2030, while making satellite maintenance and increased longevity a given. If those goals are achieved, space exploration may one day become sustainable.

477 words

Mitsunobu Okada

Notes

ℓ 20 **NASA:** National Aeronautics and Space Administration; a government agency of the US responsible for science and technology related to airplanes and space

3 |  Organizer

Complete the organizer based on the information from the reading.

Space Junk

Definition	millions of pieces of [1] _____
Size	from [2] _____ to [3] _____ _____ and even [4] _____
Speed	8 km per second

Satellites

Usage	Practical Issue
• communication ➜ [5] _____, [6] _____, and [7] _____ _____ • weather forecasts • [8] _____, etc.	increase in satellites in orbit ➜ will exponentially increase the potential for [9] _____ ➜ cascading effect ([10] _____ Syndrome): even more debris and then more collisions

Cleaning Up Space Junk (Mitsunobu Okada)

2013	He founded Astroscale, but [11] _____ _____ .
2021	His team at Astroscale succeeded in [12] _____ _____ .

Mitsunobu Okada

Sustainable Space Exploration

The UN's request	[13] _____ after 25 years.
The reality	Most satellites are left stranded and discarded.

The discussion has shifted from the removal of space junk to satellite maintenance. ***However...***

Okada's goals	• to [14] _____ by 2030 • to make [15] _____ _____ a given **Hopeful result:** Space exploration may become sustainable.

PHASE 3

◀ 2nd Viewing

Watch the video again and write down the answers to the following questions.

1. How is the cascading effect of debris explained in the video?

_____

_____

2. What idea to clean up the space junk is introduced in the video?

_____

_____

3. What is the political problem mentioned by Professor Hugh Lewis?

_____

_____

PHASE 4

💬✓ Output Task (Writing / Speaking)

You have learned that space junk can be a threat and efforts are being made to remove it from space. Let's consider some of the methods that have been proposed so far to remove space junk.

Step 1 ▶ The following are some possible ways to remove space debris. Choose one method that seems interesting to you and research it more in detail.

How to Remove Space Debris

1. Space net   A huge net captures the debris and drags it into the atmosphere where it burns up.

2. Magnet   A magnet is used to capture and drag the debris into the atmosphere where it burns up.

3. Laser   A laser beam changes the orbit of the debris so that it enters the atmosphere and burns up.

4. Tether   A special rope is used to catch the debris and guide it into the atmosphere where it burns up.

• **Which of the four methods are you interested in?** _____

• **Your Findings:** _____

_____

Hints for your research

• Has the method been demonstrated so far? If so, by what company/organization?

• Is the method safer/more economical than the other methods?

Advanced

Step 2 ▸ Find a partner and exchange the information from your research in Step 1. Think of possible features that make the methods attractive. After that, write about the method that seems the most attractive to you.

• **Which method is the most attractive to you?** _____

• **Why is it attractive?** _____

_____

_____

Step 3 ▸ Imagine you are a representative of a company that removes space junk. In a group, take turns and make a sales pitch about your technology. After everyone has finished, discuss which representative made the most convincing sales pitch.

Various methods have been proposed to remove space debris so far, but I'd say the most

attractive method of all is _____ .

Let me explain how the method works. _____
                                      (State how the method works.)

_____ .

This method is the most attractive because _____
                                           (Emphasize one feature that makes the technology attractive.)

_____ .

In short, _____ .
          (Sum up.)

📋 **Presentation Checklist**

☐ The technology is clearly described.

☐ An attractive feature of the technology is provided.

☐ Strategies (body language, eye contact, etc.) are used to grab the audience's attention.

I ♥ NY:
An Enduring Legacy of Design

We see and hear advertisements every day on TV, in magazines, on billboards, and on the radio. They're in the mail, on TV, and even personalized on our phone apps. Although we often give very little thought to ads, a great deal of thought is put into creating them. Milton Glaser's "I ♥ NY" image is a powerful example of advertising genius.

PHASE 1

1 | Getting into the Topic

The following shows two US city slogans. Fill in the blanks with the appropriate words to match with the definitions given below. Some letters for each word are given.

Famous City Slogans

Slogan		History
"The Sweetest Place on Earth"		Hershey, PA: Since the 1990s, Hershey has been ¹(p r _ _ _ t _ _ _) itself as the "Sweetest Place on Earth" because it has the famous Hershey factory, which makes world-²(r e _ _ _ n _ d) chocolate.
"I ♥ NY"		New York, NY: The ³(l _ _ _) was created in 1976 by ⁴(g _ _ _ h _ _) designer Miton Glaser. It was part of the government's efforts to attract more people to the city.

Definitions

1. to make something more popular by advertising it
2. famous and highly honored for something
3. a design or symbol used for advertising
4. connected with drawing, printing or designing

Watch the video and write down the answers to the following questions.

1. What part of the "I ♥ NY" image does the first speaker like?

_____

2. What is Milton Glaser's slogan for global warming?

_____

PHASE 2

1 📋 Vocabulary

Match the words with their definitions.

1. tiny	[ ]	**a.**	the state of being away from other people
2. bruised	[ ]	**b.**	interest or concern about something
3. awareness	[ ]	**c.**	the part of a person that judges if an action or thought is morally right or wrong
4. evoke	[ ]		
5. isolation	[ ]	**d.**	having a type of injury appearing as a discolored patch of skin
6. wit	[ ]	**e.**	very small
7. conscience	[ ]	**f.**	a kind of cleverness that mixes both intelligence and humor
		g.	to make someone think of a certain thing or feel a certain way

2 📖 Reading

Read the following passage.

Milton Glaser: The Man Who Influenced the World with Logos

According to marketing experts, the average American sees between 4,000 and 10,000 advertisements every day. This includes TV commercials, advertising boards, and the digital advertisements that come into view every time we use our smartphones or computers. Our

4 clothes, shoes, and food packages are also covered in logos to advertise the companies that

5   make them. Of course, most people only remember a tiny percentage of the advertisements they see. That is why it is important for designers to create truly memorable ones.

One man who has succeeded in creating one of the world's best-known brand logos is Milton Glaser. He created the "I ♥ NY" logo that can be found on goods sold in souvenir shops all over New York. His iconic slogan was created in 1976 as part of a campaign to promote
10 tourism in the city. In those days, the crime rate was high in New York, and residents were moving out of the city in large numbers. Glaser wanted a design that said, "I want to make this city better," and that is how the famous logo was born. His slogan resonated even more after the 9/11 terrorist attacks that saw the collapse of the World Trade Center. In the days after the attacks, Glaser updated his logo, adding the words "more than ever" and replacing the
15 red heart with a bruised one. His students from the School of Visual Arts, where he worked, distributed posters of the new version of the logo to stores all over the city. The new logo expressed the continuing love the residents had for their city.

In 2014, Glaser launched a new campaign to raise awareness about climate change. The poster consisted of the slogan "IT'S NOT WARMING, IT'S DYING" in a thick, black font
20 above a large, dark circle that was green at the bottom, fading into black at the top. Glaser believes that the language we use needs to be changed. The word "warming," he thinks, is not threatening enough and does not fully express the dangers we face.

On June 26, 2020, Glaser died at the age of 91, but until his death, he was working on a graphic project to evoke the idea of "togetherness" at a time when many New Yorkers felt
25 forced into isolation due to the COVID-19 pandemic. It was a graphical treatment of just the simple word "Together." Clearly, his lifelong belief that people can connect through art underlies this last piece of his work. Glaser's works, ranging from record covers and posters to the interior design of restaurants and their tableware, speak powerfully of the time they were created. However, they can also resonate in
30 people's hearts across generations. An obituary article by a Guardian editor described his work this way: "His America is full of colour and wit. It is playful and it has a conscience."   475 words

─────── ✎ ───────

Notes

ℓ 15 **School of Visual Arts (SVA):** a college in New York City, NY that teaches art and design

ℓ 30 **obituary:** a short article about someone's life and achievements that is printed in a newspaper soon after they have died

3 | 📄 Organizer

Complete the organizer based on the information from the reading.

Milton Glaser
(Graphic Designer)

The world of advertising

The average American sees between [1]_____ advertisements every day.

• [2]_____ of the advertisements are remembered.

• Importance of creating [3]_____

List of Glaser's works

Design	Facts and stories behind it
I ♥ NY	• Created in 1976 when the crime rate was high, and residents were [4]_____ • Part of a campaign to [5]_____ in New York
I ♥ NY [6]_____	• Created after the 9/11 terrorist attacks in 2001 • Expressed [7]_____ _____
IT'S NOT WARMING, IT'S DYING	• Created in 2014 • Part of a campaign to [8]_____ _____
Together	• Created at a time when many New Yorkers felt [9]_____ _____ • Evoked the idea of "togetherness"

Why Glaser's works are loved for so long

They [10]_____ across generations.

• An obituary article in *the Guardian*:

"His America is [11]_____. It is playful and it has a conscience."

PHASE 3

◼◀ 2nd Viewing

online video

Watch the video again and write down the answers to the following questions.

1. What are the three parts to the "I ♥ NY" puzzle?

_____

2. What message did Glaser want to spread through his "I ♥ NY" image? Name at least one.

_____

3. What is Glaser's ultimate goal for the "It's Not Warming, It's Dying" image?

_____

_____

PHASE 4

💬◀ Output Task (Writing / Speaking)

We have learned that good slogans can leave a great impression on people. Come up with your own campaign slogan to raise awareness about an issue you care about.

Step I ▶ Write down three issues that you want to eliminate. Create a slogan for each issue.

	(Issue)	(Slogan)
Example	Food waste	→ Save on Food and Save the Planet
1		→
2		→
3		→

Step 2 Choose one of the slogans you created. Then, find a partner and share your slogan with them. Make sure to do all of the following.

 Presenter

1. Explain the issue/problem.
2. Present your slogan.
3. Explain how your slogan can solve the issue.
4. Edit your slogan based on the feedback from the listener.

 Listener

1. Use descriptive adjectives (e.g., effective, catchy, dull, confusing, etc.) to give your opinion(s) of the slogan.
2. Give advice on how it can be improved.

Step 3 After editing your slogan with your partner, write a letter to your local government asking for permission to advertize your slogan. Make sure to inculde the following information.

- What is the issue *and* why is it a problem?
- What is your slogan?
- Where/how would you spread the slogan?
- What do you aim to achieve with this slogan?

Dear Governor _____ ,

   I am writing this letter to _____

_____

_____

_____

_____

                             Sincerely,

                             _____

Useful Expressions

- In order to *do what*, *who* needs to *do what (method)*.
- The best way to *do what* is to *do what (method)*.
- By *doing what*, *who* can *make what happen*.

Choosing to Be Childfree

Women are blessed with the ability to have children … at least, that's what has always been said. And while for many, having children and being a mother is a wonderful gift, it is also a huge responsibility. It is hard and stressful work and some women just aren't interested.

PHASE 1

1 | Getting into the Topic

The following are the results of a 2021 survey of approximately 4,000 US non-parents under the age of 50. Fill in the blanks with the options from a–c that you think best fit.

Why don't you want children? (Respondents who did not answer are not shown)

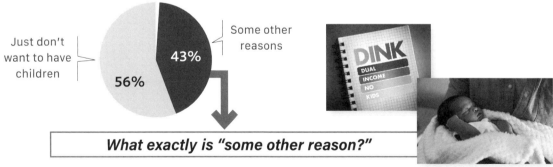

Just don't want to have children

Some other reasons

43%

56%

What exactly is "some other reason?"

1. _____ (19%)
2. _____ (17%)
3. _____ (15%)
4. Age (10%)
5. State of the world (9%)
⋮

a. Medical reasons
b. No partner
c. Financial reasons

Source: Pew Research Center

 **2**  **1st Viewing**

 online / video

Watch the video and write down the answers to the following questions.

1. According to Julia, how does the world see childfree women?

_____

2. Of the four women in the video, how many are younger than 40?

_____

PHASE 2

1 Vocabulary

Match the words with their definitions.

1. evolve   [   ]   **a.** the quality of being able to bear children

2. nanny   [   ]   **b.** to discard or leave something

3. pursue   [   ]   **c.** a person who is employed to take care of children

4. criticism   [   ]   **d.** to develop over time into something better or superior

5. narcissistic   [   ]   **e.** having or showing more than normal love or admiration for oneself

6. fertility   [   ]   **f.** to follow or work towards something, especially a goal or career

7. abandon   [   ]   **g.** harsh or judgmental remarks on someone or something's quality

2 Reading   🎧 DL 13   ⊙ CD2-06

Read the following passage.

The Childfree Choice

     In many cultures, in spite of the evolving roles that women have played in society, a young woman's goal in life was often thought to be to find a husband and have children. Today, however, more and more women are openly saying that they do not want children.

4   Unfortunately, not everyone accepts this new way of thinking, and many women have had to

defend their choice, especially against the opposition of their families and friends. Although their reasons are various, there is a definite trend toward "childfree" womanhood.

One reason for living childfree is the stress of childcare. As Julia (36), a woman who was interviewed by *the Guardian*, explained, she loved children and enjoyed working as a teacher and nanny. However, her experiences caring for children taught her how stressful and tiring childcare was. Meanwhile, other women such as Altagracia (30) and Kristen (45) simply never felt the desire to have children. Changes in society have also contributed to the childfree phenomenon. The development of contraceptives and contraceptive practices has helped women delay pregnancy and thus pursue careers, while the increase in career opportunities and access to higher education for women have given women more freedom and opportunities that traditionally only men had.

In spite of being childfree for almost all the same reasons as men, these women have been met with criticism. Surprisingly, it is other women who tend to criticize this choice the most; childfree women are called "selfish" and "narcissistic" for not wanting to have kids. It also seems that family and friends are often opposed to the choice to live childfree, and many argue that children are lovely and that a life without children is lonely. One of the most common arguments against going childfree is that the person will regret that choice later in life.

Young women are often reminded of the "ticking clock," and are told at the early stages of their careers that they must have children soon "before it's too late." However, society's views seem to be changing. In one example, the president of an all-female college at the University of Cambridge was heavily criticized by the media when she introduced "fertility lessons" that taught female students to start planning for children by their mid-thirties. It is clear that although many people still struggle to accept women's choice to be childfree, society has abandoned the idea that children must be a part of a woman's life goals. In spite of the opposition from their surroundings, women today are making their voices heard. The desire to have children, the ability to have children, and the options for how and when to have children are now issues for each individual to consider for herself. With or without support, various changes have made it possible for women to choose their own life paths.

469 words

Notes

-free: without the thing mentioned (for example, "childfree" means without child[ren])

ℓ 12 **contraceptive:** (of a drug, device or practice) used to prevent a woman from becoming pregnant

ℓ 23 **ticking clock:** a phrase often used to express a lack of time or a time limit approaching

3 📄 Organizer

Complete the organizer based on the information from the reading.

Women's Goals

Past	**A young woman's goal in life:** to ¹ _____
Today	**More women are openly saying** ² _____ Reasons for this choice: • Childcare can be stressful and ³ _____ . • They never felt ⁴ _____ . ⎡Changes in society⎤ • The development of ⁵ _____ has helped women delay pregnancy and thus pursue careers. • The increase in ⁶ _____ _____ have given women more freedom and opportunities.

Criticism

From whom?	Other ⁷ _____ / Friends and family
What?	• Called "⁸ _____" and "⁹ _____" for not wanting to have kids • Children are ¹⁰ _____ _____ .

Changing Society

• Abandoned the idea that ¹¹ _____ .
  e.g., The President of an all-female college at the University of Cambridge was heavily criticized
  by the media when she introduced "¹² _____ "
• Women are now having their voices heard.
• Various changes have made it possible for ¹³ _____
_____ .

PHASE 3

◼◀ 2nd Viewing

Watch the video again and write down the answers to the following questions.

1. Why doesn't Kristen want to have children?

_____

2. Where are Altagracia's parents from?

_____

3. Julia said "there are lots of other things that make a woman a woman." What two examples did she give?

_____

PHASE 4

💬✎ Output Task (Writing / Speaking)

As you now know, some people choose to be childfree.
Discuss the benefits and drawbacks of having children today.

Step 1 ▶ Find a partner and together, list some of the reasons that people choose to have children and some of the reasons they choose not to have children. Make sure to consider reasons for both men and women. You may use your own knowledge and what you have learned.

Reasons to have children	Reasons not to have children

Advanced

Step 2 Now, imagine you work for your university's student magazine. Fill in the below outline of an article informing students of the benefits and drawbacks of having children today.

Opening Sentence	There are both benefits and drawbacks to having children today.
Transition	First,
Benefits	
Transition	Now, let's move on to
Drawbacks	
Closing Sentence(s)	(restating the opening sentence with different wording, summarizing your points, describing today's society, etc.)

Step 3 Exchange articles with your partner. Evaluate your partner's article based on the checklist below. Then, share and discuss your feedback.

Checklist

☐ The article gave convincing reasons for both having and not having children.

☐ The article gave me a new way of thinking.

☐ I found the information in the article useful.

"Comments/Feedback"

Shedding Light on Black Cowboy History

The common image of cowboys comes from the white cowboy heroes in the Westerns. However, the cowboy culture actually began with black cowboys. To understand this gap between our image and reality, you would have to look at the history of cowboys. Although the need for cowboys has declined today, the black cowboy culture still remains alive.

PHASE 1

1 | Getting into the Topic

Meet Larry Callies, the operator of the Black Cowboy Museum in Texas, US. Read what he says about his life and arrange the words in the brackets in the correct order.

⊙ **Tell us a little about yourself.**

I come from a long line of cowboy myself. When I was young, I ¹[be / a country music singer/ until / used to] I quit after problems with my vocal cords. Now I am the operator of the Black Cowboy Museum in Texas.

⊙ **What made you decide to start the Black Cowboy Museum?**

When I worked at a ranch outside Houston, I ²[to find / of cowboys / photographs / happened] from the 1880s. All of them were black, just like me. So I began to collect saddles, boots, and sheriff pins that once belonged to black cowboys, and with these collections, I opened the museum in 2017. My mission is to ³[the hidden history / the public / let / know] of black cowboys.

1. _____

2. _____

3. _____

2 1st Viewing

Watch the video and write down the answers to the following questions.

1. Who was the term "cowboy" actually reserved specifically for?

_____

2. Whose real story does the Western (a movie genre) titled *The Searchers* come from?

_____

PHASE 2

1 📋 Vocabulary

Match the words with their definitions.

1. **bandit**   [   ]   **a.** a person who keeps animals such as cows and horses at a farm

2. **criminal**   [   ]   **b.** to make a law ineffective

3. **tend**   [   ]   **c.** to make things look in a way that unfairly favors white people

4. **emerge**   [   ]   **d.** to take care of something

5. **abolish**   [   ]   **e.** a person who does illegal things

6. **rancher**   [   ]   **f.** to come to be known or exist

7. **whitewash**   [   ]   **g.** a robber who attacks travelers

2 📖 Reading

 DL 14   CD2-07

Read the following passage.

The Black Cowboy: Rewriting the Whitewashed History of American Heroes

What kind of person do you imagine the typical American cowboy to be? For most people, it would be a white man on a horse, wearing a wide-brimmed hat and carrying a pistol. It certainly would not be a man like Lil Nas X, one of the most influential black rappers today, who appeared riding a horse in the official video of his blockbuster single

5   *Old Town Road*. However, Lil Nas X is actually closer to the true image of a cowboy than you might expect. The cowboy boots and hat he was wearing in the video are a symbol of a

forgotten part of African American history—that of the black cowboy.

The classic figure of the white cowboy comes from the "Westerns," a genre of action movie that was popular from the 1930s to the 1960s. The traditional hero of the Westerns was the cowboy, who would engage in gunfights with Native Americans or an assortment of bandits and criminals and save the day. Perhaps the most famous actor of the genre was John Wayne. He appeared in classic movies such as *Red River* (1948) and *The Searchers* (1956), which are often cited as the best Westerns of all time. However, it is a little-known fact that *The Searchers* was actually based on the story of a black cowboy called Britt Johnson, who is said to have bravely pursued a group of Native Americans who had captured his family.

In fact, historians estimate that around one in four cowboys were black. The history of black cowboys dates back to the 19th century, when white Americans moved to Texas with their black slaves, seeking vast land for cattle ranches. It is said that while the white men were away fighting in the Civil War, the black slaves had diligently tended their masters' cows, which were at the heart of the Texas cattle industry. This is when the black cowboy—boy who looked after cows—emerged. Even after slavery was abolished, white ranchers brought skilled black cowboys back to maintain their land. Although most of these cowboys probably did not see much thrilling action like Britt Johnson had, they were still heroes in their own right, working hard at a job that most white ranchers simply could not handle themselves.

Even after the need for cowboys started to decline, the public remained fascinated by the cowboy, and thus, rodeos were introduced. Among many others, the Bill Picket Rodeo, which is a specifically black rodeo, holds special meaning for black people. It was named after a legendary black cowboy and celebrates the men and women of color who keep the cowboy tradition alive. Black horse-riding groups across the country also work to make horse-riding more accessible to everyone. Their aim is to combat stereotypes and teach the true history of the cowboy, which has been whitewashed by Hollywood for so long.

480 words

Notes

ℓ 12 **save the day:** to manage to make something end successfully in a situation where it was likely to fail

ℓ 13 *Red River* **(1948):** the story of a young cowhand who rebels against his adoptive stepfather

ℓ 13 *The Searchers* **(1956):** the story of a Civil War veteran who travels to find his niece who was captured by a Native American tribe

ℓ 20 **the (American) Civil War:** A war in the US in 1861–1865. It was fought between the northern industrial states, which were against slavery, and the southern agricultural states, which wanted to keep slavery.

ℓ 28 **rodeo:** a sport and public entertainment in which cowboys show different skills by riding wild horses and catching cows with ropes

3 📄 Organizer

Complete the organizer based on the information from the reading.

Images of Cowboys

| Common image | a white man on a horse, wearing [1] _____ and carrying [2] _____ |

• **Lil Nas X** (appeared in a music video in a cowboy costume)

close to [3] _____

• **The classic cowboy figures from Westerns**

— Cowboys engaged in [4] _____ with Native Americans or an assortment of

[5] _____

— Famous actor = [6] _____ (appeared in *Red River* and *The Searchers*)

> **However...**

• A little-known fact is that *The Searchers* was based on [7] _____

_____ .

• Historians estimate that [8] _____ .

The True History of Cowboys

• **19th century:**

— White Americans moved to Texas with [9] _____ .

— While the white men were away fighting in the Civil War, the slaves [10] _____

_____ (= at the heart of the Texas cattle industry).

• **After slavery was abolished:**

White ranchers brought [11] _____

_____ .

• **After the decline in the need for cowboys:**

— People remained fascinated by the cowboy ➔ [12] _____ were introduced.

e.g., all-black Bill Picket Rodeo

— Black horse-riding groups work to make horse-riding more accessible to everyone

└Their aim: To combat [13] _____ and teach

[14] _____ of the cowboy

PHASE 3

▣◀ 2nd Viewing

Watch the video again and write down the answers to the following questions.

1. By 1860, what percentage of Texans were slaves?

_____

2. What did Bass Reeves, the real lone ranger, do in his lifetime?

_____

3. What kind of event is the "Bill Pickett Rodeo"?

_____

_____

PHASE 4

💬✍ Output Task (Writing / Speaking)

You have learned that movies had a part in whitewashing the history of cowboys. Let's have a look at other cases of whitewashing in movies.

Step 1 ▶ Many films featuring white actors as the main heroes have been criticized of whitewashing. Research the following example and fill in the blank in the table. Then, find an example of whitewashed films and write down the following information on the next page.

Title	Plot	Character(s)
The Great Wall (2016)	European merchants travel to ancient China in search of black powder. However, they get involved in fights against monsters. The main character plays a heroic role in helping the Chinese army fight against the monsters.	_____ plays the main character, who has excellent skills in shooting arrows and plays an important role in the battles.

- *Advanced*

- **Title:** _____

- **The Main Character:** _____
  (Who plays the main character? What is his/her race?)

- **Plot:** _____
  _____

Step 2 Find a partner and introduce the film you researched. Then, discuss why whitewashing is a problem.

> **Why whitewashing is a problem**
>
> —Write down possible drawbacks of whitewashed movies from these points of view.
>
> → Drawbacks for actors/entertainment world
>
> → Drawbacks for society

Step 3 Find another pair and plan a presentation based on the information from Steps 1 and 2. Introduce the title and plot of the movie as well as the characters played by white actors. Include your opinion on the impacts of whitewashing.

I researched a movie titled _____.

It's about _____.
(Briefly summarize the movie [plot, characters, etc.].)

In my opinion, _____.
(Possible impacts of whitewashing)

I hope that _____.
(Your future prospect of the issue)

Presentation Checklist

☐ The basic information about the movie (title, characters, etc.) is clearly stated.

☐ A concise description of the plot is provided.

☐ Opinions are clearly stated on the impacts of whitewashing.

Women Finding Their Strength

Femininity [noun]: the qualities or attributes regarded as characteristic of women. Many people still think this means being delicate and sensitive, and liking flowery dresses. But not *everone* thinks so. For some, it is about being strong and independent inside and out. Is femininity changing? And if so, how?

PHASE 1

| 1 | Getting into the Topic

Read the following blog post by a female college student and put the underlined words into the correct word form.

Thoughts about our girls' night out   *Posted: 11:00 PM 3h ago*

I had fun (as always), but was a bit embarrassed last night.
My friends kept talking about the Instagrammers they're hooked on right now.
When I said, "they're a bit too skinny, aren't they," my friends started laughing at me and told me I'd be more **¹attract** and feminine if I lost weight.

Hmm…feminine.

This made me wonder what **²feminine** really means to me. Should everyone aim for model-like **³thin**? I mean, I'm not super-skinny, but I like to go to the gym and build a bit of muscle. It gives me **⁴satisfy** to be able to be in control of my body.

Ah, whatever! I'm probably fine as I am…no matter what my friends say!
I'll think about this some more tomorrow. For now, good night!

1._____ 2._____ 3._____ 4._____

2 | ◀ 1st Viewing

online video

Watch the video and write down the answers to the following questions.

1. Previous to bodybuilding, what did Rene Campbell do?

_____

2. While in Gran Canaria, what family event did Rene Campbell miss?

_____

PHASE 2

1 | 📋 Vocabulary

Match the words with their definitions.

1. **aspire**	[ ]	**a.** an unfounded negative opinion about someone/something
2. **take up**	[ ]	**b.** different from the way most people behave and/or think
3. **strain**	[ ]	**c.** something (i.e., a task, system, relationship, etc.) that makes you feel nervous because it is demanding
4. **unforgiving**	[ ]	
5. **prejudice**	[ ]	**d.** unpleasant or causing great difficulty
6. **unconventional**	[ ]	**e.** to learn or start to do something, especially for pleasure or as a job
7. **toned**	[ ]	**f.** to want to gain or become something
		g. having firm and well-defined muscles

2 | 📖 Reading

 DL 15 CD2-08

Read the following passage.

Feminine Macho: Redefining Beauty and Strength

At 88 kg and with a muscular chest measuring over 120 cm (about 15 cm more than the average man), bodybuilder Rene Campbell is not what most people would consider traditionally feminine. In her youth, Rene (now in her 40s) aspired to the stick-thin cover-model body, struggling with eating disorders for many years. One day, however, a live
5 bodybuilding contest changed her life. She was mesmerized by the strong, muscular bodies

on stage and the confidence that the contestants showed, standing in front of a large crowd wearing only miniscule bikinis. She decided to take up bodybuilding herself, and she became a professional bodybuilder in 2013. Although she has faced other challenges since then, she claims that she is more confident about her body than ever before.

10   For the professional bodybuilder, preparation is a full-time job. In addition to training hard every day, Rene must control every calorie she puts into her body. In order to take in enough protein to build muscle, she eats a kilogram of chicken spread over five meals a day. Most bodybuilders go through phases of "bulking," during which they over-eat to build muscle, and "cutting," during which they get rid of fat by eating very little. Although this

15 makes the bodybuilders' massive muscles stand out the way they do, it also puts considerable strain on their bodies and can be dangerous. Rene has also had to sacrifice her marriage and precious time with her children to achieve her bodybuilding goals.

    On top of dealing with the unforgiving nature of bodybuilding itself, Rene is also fighting a social battle. In an interview with CNN, she explained that she received cruel

20 comments from people who did not understand why women would want to be muscular, even once being asked to leave the women's toilets because she looked "too masculine." Rene and other female bodybuilders work to break down this sort of prejudice because, although unconventional, they believe in a different kind of beauty and their right to pursue it. While bodybuilding is not particularly healthy, it is controlled. Women who have struggled with

25 lack of control over themselves and their bodies, especially after a traumatic experience, alcoholism, or an eating disorder, are particularly drawn to this profession, as it allows them to fully "own" themselves.

    In recent years, social media has also helped in changing the ideal female body image. Instead of model-like thinness, a sporty, toned physique is what many women aspire to

30 today. Social media is littered with photos of women working out, followed by hashtags such as #fitspiration and #shesquats. For people like Rene Campbell who go one step further, bodybuilding is about both strength and beauty. It is a lifestyle choice and an art. Although bodybuilding is not easy, Rene has gained a sense of confidence and mental strength through her

35 work, and is proud to be who she is.   478 words

Notes

  ℓ 3   **cover model:** a person who is put on the front cover of a magazine, or who looks like such a person

  ℓ 12 **protein:** a nutrient found largely in meats and an essential part of body structures (e.g., muscle, hair, etc.)

  ℓ 29 **physique:** the size and shape of a person's body

3 | 📄 Organizer

Complete the organizer based on the information from the reading.

Rene Campbell: The Life of a Female Bodybuilder

Background	• **Weight:** [1]_____ kg / • **Chest size:** [2]_____ cm / • **Age:** 40s • **Occupation:** bodybuilder ↑ Inspiration: watching [3]_____

Training Challenges	• **Main daily activity:** [4]_____
	• **How to build massive muscles:**
	  — **Meals:** have 1kg of chicken spread over [5]_____
	  — **Bulking:** over-eating
	  — **Cutting:** [6]_____
	    → puts [7]_____
	• **What Rene has sacrificed:** [8]_____
	    _____

Social Challenges	• **Main challenges:** fighting [9]_____
	  — comments from people who do not understand women's desire to be muscular
	  — asked to leave [10]_____
	
	↕
	
	• **Rene and other female bodybuilders:**
	  — They believe in [11]_____ and their
	    right to pursue it.
	  — Women who [12]_____
	    _____
	    tend to be drawn to bodybuilding.

⬇

Recent Changes	• **Change in society's views on the ideal female body:** Many women aspire to [13]_____ today. —Photos with #fitspiration and #shesquats on social media

PHASE 3

◼◁ 2nd Viewing

(online video)

Watch the video again and write down the answers to the following questions.

1. Previous to starting bodybuilding, what sort of person was Rene?

_____

2. What happens to Rene when she goes into the gym?

_____

3. Why wouldn't Rene stop training even when her doctor advised her to get rid of her muscles?

_____

PHASE 4

💬✎ Output Task (Writing / Speaking)

Rene Campbell challenges the stereotype of femininity by bodybuilding and choosing a muscular physique. However, there are many other gender stereotypes, for both men and women, that can cause problems. Discuss the gender stereotypes in today's society and how to challenge them.

Step I ▶ Find a partner and think of some stereotypes of femininity and masculinity. List at least two in each column below. List at least one that does not relate to looks or physical features.

Femininity	Masculinity

Step 2 Find a partner and choose one stereotype from Step 1 to discuss. Then, write down what you have learned about common gender stereotypes.

 You may ask your partner questions such as:

- What is a good example of how/where this stereotype can be seen today?
- What are some exceptions to this stereotype?
- How can people challenge/are people challenging the stereotype?

   e.g., My grandmother keeps trying to teach me how to sew/knit/embroider, but I don't think I need this skill …

   Whenever I cry watching a movie, my father tells me "boys don't cry," but I don't agree …

Common gender stereotypes

Example	
How to challenge it	

Step 3 Write an opinion article about whether or not you think the stereotype is changing. Then, make a few suggestions for what can be done to change the stereotype in the future. Use the examples you came up with to explain your position.

_____

_____

_____

_____

_____

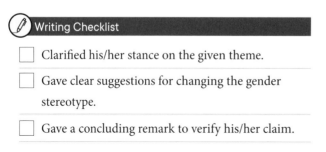

Writing Checklist

☐ Clarified his/her stance on the given theme.

☐ Gave clear suggestions for changing the gender stereotype.

☐ Gave a concluding remark to verify his/her claim.

Useful Expressions

- In my opinion, …
- Although …
- In order to *do what (aim)*, *who* can try *doing what (method)*.

Video Credit

Unit 1   University, students clash over 'hazing' nicknames (September 5, 2014)
www.theguardian.com/world/video/2014/sep/05/university-western-sydney-bans-hazing-hoodies-nicknames

Unit 2   The Green Recovery: how Australia can ditch coal (August 26, 2020)
www.theguardian.com/australia-news/video/2020/aug/27/the-green-recovery-how-australia-can-ditch-coal-without-ditching-jobs

Unit 3   The colour of power: why is the British establishment so white? (September 25, 2017)
www.theguardian.com/inequality/video/2017/sep/25/the-colour-of-power-why-is-the-british-establishment-so-white

Unit 4   She's not perfect. But could it still work? (April 1, 2015)
www.theguardian.com/lifeandstyle/video/2015/apr/01/shes-not-perfect-but-could-it-still-work-philippa-perry-video

Unit 5   Why forcing cyclists to wear helmets will not save lives (May 31, 2018)
www.theguardian.com/lifeandstyle/video/2018/may/31/why-forcing-cyclists-to-wear-helmets-will-not-save-lives-video-explainer

Unit 6   Making carbon-neutral clothes out of algae: the designers taking on fast fashion (September 20, 2019)
www.theguardian.com/fashion/video/2019/sep/20/algae-threads-over-cotton-clothes-how-fashion-is-going-green-video

Unit 7   Testing the waters: what we learned from a 'water sommelier' (February 19, 2015)
www.theguardian.com/us-news/video/2015/feb/19/water-tasting-water-sommelier-video

Unit 8   Need a mom? Help is at hand with one woman's new service (November 9, 2015)
www.theguardian.com/world/video/2015/nov/09/need-a-mom-help-is-at-hand-with-one-woman-new-service-video

Unit 9   Robots can predict the future … and so can you (February 2, 2017)
www.theguardian.com/lifeandstyle/video/2017/feb/02/robots-can-predict-the-future-and-so-can-you-video

Unit 10   No TV, no sat nav, no internet: how to fix space's junk problem (April 1, 2020)
www.theguardian.com/science/video/2020/apr/01/no-tv-no-sat-nav-no-internet-how-to-fix-spaces-junk-problem-video

Unit 11   Anyone who lives in New York will see it 100 times a day: meet Milton Glaser, the creator of the 'I love NY' logo (September 20, 2014)
www.theguardian.com/artanddesign/video/2014/sep/20/i-love-ny-milton-glaser-logo

Unit 12   Being childfree: five women on why they chose not to have kids (July 7, 2020)
www.theguardian.com/us-news/video/2020/jul/07/being-childfree-four-women-on-why-they-chose-not-to-have-kids-video

Unit 13   Why the first US cowboys were black (October 29, 2020)
www.theguardian.com/culture/video/2020/oct/29/why-the-first-us-cowboys-were-black

Unit 14   It's my body of armour: my life as a female bodybuilder (October 21, 2015)
www.theguardian.com/news/video/2015/oct/21/strength-power-femininity-female-bodybuilder-video

Photo Credit

このテキストのメインページ
www.kinsei-do.co.jp/plusmedia/417

次のページの QR コードを読み取ると
直接ページにジャンプできます

オンライン映像配信サービス「plus⁺Media」について

本テキストの映像は plus⁺Media ページ（www.kinsei-do.co.jp/plusmedia）から、ストリーミング再生でご利用いただけます。手順は以下に従ってください。

ログイン

●ご利用には、ログインが必要です。
　サイトのログインページ（www.kinsei-do.co.jp/plusmedia/login）へ行き、plus⁺Media パスワード（次のページのシールをはがしたあとに印字されている数字とアルファベット）を入力します。

●パスワードは各テキストにつき１つです。
　有効期限は、はじめてログインした時点から１年間になります。

ログインページ

[利用方法]

次のページにある QR コード、もしくは plus⁺Media トップページ（www.kinsei-do.co.jp/plusmedia）から該当するテキストを選んで、そのテキストのメインページにジャンプしてください。

メニューページ　　　　　再生画面

plus⁺Media トップ　　　メインページ

「Video」「Audio」をタッチすると、それぞれのメニューページにジャンプしますので、そこから該当する項目を選べば、ストリーミングが開始されます。

[推奨環境]

iOS (iPhone, iPad)	OS: iOS 12 以降 ブラウザ：標準ブラウザ	Android	OS: Android 6 以降 ブラウザ：標準ブラウザ、Chrome
PC	OS: Windows 7/8/8.1/10, MacOS X　ブラウザ：Internet Explorer 10/11, Microsoft Edge, Firefox 48以降, Chrome 53以降, Safari		

※最新の推奨環境についてはウェブサイトをご確認ください。
※上記の推奨環境を満たしている場合でも、機種によってはご利用いただけない場合もあります。また、推奨環境は技術動向等により変更される場合があります。予めご了承ください。

このシールをはがすと
plus+Media 利用のための
パスワードが
記載されています。

一度はがすと元に戻すことは
できませんのでご注意下さい。

◀ ここからはがして下さい

4176 INTEGRITY
Advanced

plus+Media

本書にはCD（別売）があります

INTEGRITY　Advanced

Vitalize Your English Studies with Authentic Videos

海外メディア映像から深める ４技能・教養英語【上級編】

2023年1月20日　初版第1刷発行
2023年2月20日　初版第2刷発行

編著者　　　竹　内　　理
　　　　　　山　岡　浩　一
　　　　　　森　安　瑞　希
　　　　　　Brent Cotsworth
発行者　　　福　岡　正　人
発行所　　株式会社　金星堂

（〒101-0051）　東京都千代田区神田神保町 3-21
Tel　　(03) 3263-3828（営業部）
　　　　(03) 3263-3997（編集部）
Fax　　(03) 3263-0716
https://www.kinsei-do.co.jp

編集担当　蔦原美智・長島吉成　　　　　　　　　　　Printed in Japan
印刷所・製本所／萩原印刷株式会社

ISBN978-4-7647-4176-8　C1082